Best Friends Worlds Apart

Ellie,
Your work is so
much a part of
my story. Enjoy
it, Gayle

Best Friends Worlds Apart

by

Gayle Peebles

For Stassya and Helen

Thank you for all the beautiful memories
you have given me. My life has been full
of love, adventure, and surprises because
of you. I hope our story will inspire others
to make friends, even if worlds apart.

ACKNOWLEDGEMENTS

To Valerie Serrano, my teacher, mentor, editor, and friend. These two years, and more, have been an inspiration to me. I could not have done this without you and the encouragement of your other students. I dedicate all my commas and *had beens* to you.

To Jim my husband, Kay Johnson my sister, and Pat Komosinski, retired high school history and social studies teacher. Thank you for taking the time to read my manuscript and offer me your invaluable suggestions. I have accepted nearly every one of them.

To all my friends, family, and cruise table-mates, I thank you for your support and undivided attention when I shared my stories. You encouraged me all the way.

To Tom and Lilka Areton. Thank you for your trust and your love for all humanity, and for inspiring those of us lucky enough to have been able to share in your quest for peace and friendship for all the world's people. In the thirty-five years I have known and worked with you, I have never seen you slow down. I suspect you never will.

Table of Contents

PART ONE: The Exchange

1. Welcome to America

[From Washington DC:]

December 1989

Dear Gayle, Stassya's letter began, *I am sitting in Washington DC's airport and waiting for my plane. Christmas tree is near me, beautiful shops in airport are open soft music, smiling and happy faces everywhere. I think I and our kids are the only gloomy ones here. We are leaving the wonderful country, kind and friendly, polite people. I hope not forever. Thanks to you, I had the most charming and happy days in my life: no worrying, no troubles, no lining up. At the airport I couldn't say a word. I tried not to look at you. I began to cry. Parting is very difficult. Even the wonders and beauty of Disneyland couldn't sweeten the bitterness of parting. We had wonderful days together. I wish we had had more free time. I like your family and the way we celebrated Xmas. Thank you my dear teacher, host mother and friend! I miss you so badly. Kiss Jim and thank all useful things, please. I love you all. Yours, Stanislava*

My first clear memory of Stassya was of her sitting in our living room on our white L-shaped sofa after she had settled into her room in our home.

The white sofa

She sat up very straight and proud. She had on very high-heeled, knee-length boots, a bright pink and black sweater with wide stripes, and a long, dark blue denim skirt. Her hair was a henna red, shoulder length, and slightly curly. She had smooth, pale skin, and big brown eyes.

She had just arrived from Leningrad, Russia, and I was curious about her. Since she was an English teacher in Russia, her English was excellent, although quite British-sounding. We were a bit shy with each other, kind of just sitting, and wondering what to say. So I thought of a question that might help us begin to talk.

"So what is happening in Russia right now?" I asked her.

Her answer was the beginning of our incredible story.

"My dahling," she said, "I must start from the beginning."

For someone like me who likes a story to have a beginning and an end, not like soap operas that never end, this was perfect. I couldn't wait, and suggested we adjourn to the dining room table for a cup of tea. That would be our place every night for three weeks while Stassya, a gifted storyteller, taught me Russian history, art, music, and literature, holding me spellbound for hours on end.

~ ~

This extraordinary experience started with my association with Cultural Homestay International (CHI), a nonprofit, national organization based in San Anselmo, California, with area administrators throughout the United States and Canada, and I was a coordinator of their homestay programs in my town. My job was to find nice, willing host families for students and their teachers—usually for two-week to three-week stays. I was to conduct classes in

13

conversational English in the mornings and plan outings in the afternoons, ranging from cultural to fun activities.

Up until 1989, my experience had only been with students from various high schools in Japan. The students had limited speaking ability in English; so I planned class activities that pushed them to overcome their shyness and begin to speak the English they had been learning in Japan.

As things began to loosen up in Russia, Tom and Lilka Areton, the founders of CHI, traveled to Russia. Tom spoke Russian fluently because he grew up in Russian-occupied Czechoslovakia. He had left his home and family in 1968 and took the train to Paris where he had waited for a visa to come to America. This happened just days before Russia had driven their tanks into Prague and closed the borders. Eventually, Tom arrived in New York and met his future wife Lilka. The two of them settled in Marin County, California, and began CHI in the hopes of promoting student exchanges.

Tom's dream was to someday begin a program with Russian students to promote the ideal of the freedom he had been denied as a child growing up in a repressive society. Thus, when the borders were eased a bit, he had headed to Moscow and Leningrad (later to become St. Petersburg) and had obtained permission to visit High School #160 in Leningrad, since they had a program of English. This would make communication easier. Tom had an agenda. He proposed receiving a group of Russian students for a homestay program in California with the idea that there would be a complete exchange of American students visiting High School #160 and staying with families there.

Stassya's classroom in HS 160 had been chosen as the meeting venue for Tom and Lilka because Stassya's room had been decorated so nicely. She was not particularly happy about staying after school to meet and entertain yet another group from abroad with refreshments and conversation; however, Stassya's deep sense of obligation had prevented her from saying no. She therefore made arrangements for her eight-year-old daughter Helen to wait for her after school, and then set about preparing some refreshments.

The homestay idea was met with enthusiasm by the staff, but they had heard this a few times in the past, and did not think too much about it at first. However, Tom made them a proposal which was accepted, then went home, and began to plan what was to be the first CHI high school exchange with Russia, for December 1989, with a return exchange of American students staying with host

14

families in Leningrad in the summer of 1990. While Tom was preparing here in the United States, the two English teachers in Russia, Stassya and Ludmilla, who had met with Tom and Lilka in Leningrad, were asked to prepare a group of Russian students to go to America, and Stassya and Ludmilla began the process of choosing the best students from their English classes. I was asked by Tom to be one of two coordinators on this side of the Atlantic, and I began to interview potential host families.

My co-teacher Marilyn and I planned our classes and outings and, by December, we were ready to welcome twenty-five Russian high school students, their two English teachers, and principal Mr. Korevsky, to America. The group traveled via Washington, DC, where it had snowed about two inches, virtually closing the city. The group thought that was hilarious and, after checking in at their hotel for a two-night stay, the group proceeded to walk all over and enjoy the sights, never mind that little bit of snow!

After visiting Washington, D.C., the students and adults arrived at San Francisco airport where they were met by the host families that had been selected from Marin Academy. We sorted them out, introduced everyone, and sent them home. My husband Jim and I took the two Russian teachers home in our car.

While driving down Market Street in the San Francisco financial district and looking through the open sunroof, Stassya and Ludmilla pointed out "the tops of the buildings". As I looked up out of my car window, I saw for the first time the unique decorations above the highest windows on the tall buildings. There were statues, arches, and bas reliefs with floral and abstract designs making each building different from the next. In all the times I'd been there, I had never noticed the tops of the buildings before. We crossed the Golden Gate Bridge to more excited exclamations from the back seat, and then drove another hour to Santa Rosa. We dropped Ludmilla off at her host-family's home in a local rural area, and took Stassya to our home in Santa Rosa.

Thus began our three-week adventure. The next day with the students sitting on chairs in a circle in our classroom at Marin Academy High School, Marilyn and I started to assess their ability to speak English. We began with asking each student to introduce themselves and state what they would like to learn while they were here.

The first question from one of the students was, "What American literature are we going to study?"

15

Marilyn looked at me and I at her. With our eyes wide and a slight grin on our faces, our expressions must have shown our surprise at their fluency in English and their eagerness to have a chance to discuss our famous authors! *Okay*, I thought to myself, *so much for our lesson plans!*

"I read Stephen King novels," Marilyn said to me. "What do you read?"

I wasn't much into the literary authors to whom the students were referring, myself, so after class we scrambled to find a "real" English Lit teacher to help us out, and we found the perfect one. The first morning she sat the surprised students on the floor in a circle, and had them enthralled every morning for the full three weeks. She even had gathered generous donations of books such as *Tom Sawyer*, *Huckleberry Finn*, *Grapes of Wrath*, and some books of Jack London (our famous local author) from various local bookstores for each student to keep as a gift. With that taken care of, Marilyn and I took charge of outings and afternoon activities.

When our first day in class came to an end, I made sure all the students were okay after their long flight, that the class had gone smoothly, that we'd all had enough to do, and that we had all bonded as students and teachers.

It was exhausting driving two hours roundtrip between Marin County and Santa Rosa every day, and then fix dinner when I got home. That first day, on our way back to Santa Rosa, I made a quick stop at the local grocery store for a few things.

When the doors parted automatically, Stassya backed up with a startled look and exclaimed, "Thank you, doors." She proudly walked right in, head up, and chin out. I asked her to pick out some lunchmeat she would like for sandwiches. She took one look around and said, "It is impossible–I have never had so many choices. You choose for me, I cannot make up my mind."

I picked out some smoked chicken and walked to the aisle with the salad dressings. I hurriedly picked up a bottle of honey mustard (my husband's favorite), and put it into my cart.

"It's time to go," I said, as I began to push the cart down the aisle. "It's getting late, and I have to prepare dinner."
I turned to be sure she was following me, and there she was looking at me with those big eyes, saying, "But, dahling, the shapes of the bahtles!"

16

2. Time Together

After studying the shapes of the bottles together, we drove up the hill to my home where I automatically opened our garage door and drove in to the chant of, "Thank you, door," from Stassya in the passenger seat beside me. I managed to keep it a secret until Stassya noticed a few days later that I was using a device she referred to as "a useful thing". We had already begun our chatting and laughing.

Dinner had been prepared the night before so I only needed the microwave to warm it. I just put together a quick salad. More than a year later, I learned that Stassya had been shocked when I grabbed a handful of cold, cooked spaghetti, plopped it on her plate, spooned out some meat sauce and some cold, cooked broccoli, and slipped the plate into the microwave oven. In less than two minutes, dinner was cooked. At that time, I didn't know that Stassya was a proficient cook and cooked everything from scratch. I, on the other hand can exist without a kitchen as I really do not enjoy cooking all that much anymore. Over the years I had cooked for a family of five, plus students who lived with us from time to time for a week or even a full school year. I had baked bread, picked blackberries and made pies and jams, baked cookies by the dozens, and even grew my own garden fruits and vegetables, which threatened to overtake the neighborhood.

But Stassya had been pleasantly surprised by my excellent spaghetti dinner, and very impressed at how quickly I could produce it on the table, hot, and perfectly cooked. She asked me to tell her about the new device I used—"the magic oven", as she called it. She mastered that in no time at all.

Our weekends were free, so I decided to take Stassya to the mall on Saturday. JC Penney was having their annual Red Tag Sale Day. Stassya had some money from friends in Russia who had asked her to do some shopping for them. Our first stop was the ATM machine to get cash for lunch. Stassya became very excited to see money coming out of the bank and into my hands by way of the wall!

"You can get money from the wall?" she said. She had not realized it was a bank—she just saw the wall handing me money. I also kept that a secret until someone later gave it away.

Next, off to JC Penney. As we entered the department store, Stassya looked around, with her eyes wide, at all the color and abundance.

"Oh, my," was her first reaction. "This is beautisome."

(I didn't realize until much later the startling contrast between our lives in the world of shopping.)

"Pick out what you like, and we will go to the dressing room and try everything on," I told her.

It didn't take her long to get the idea, so we began to grab armloads of tops, bottoms, dresses, sweaters, and a lot more. We had dressing rooms next to each other with curtains hung across the openings. I could hear Stassya humming and hangers rattling.

"Let me know when you try on the two-piece black and white dress," I said as I poked my head out from behind my curtain.

"I'm ready," she called out.

I quickly grabbed my black and white two pieces and slipped them on, zipping and buttoning as I stepped out from behind the curtain.

"We match!" I exclaimed as we looked in the mirror. The dresses were black with tiny white flowers, had a dainty white crocheted collar, and pearly buttons down the front. We smiled at our reflection, gave each other a hug, and both decided on those dresses.

"What else are you going to buy?" I asked.

"All of them," she immediately answered.

"Me, too," I said as we gathered up our loads and headed to the cash register.

When we got home with all our packages, we modeled our matching dresses for my husband Jim. He grabbed the camera and captured two happy ladies posing with delighted grins on their faces not realizing the importance that simple click of the camera would have for us, years later.

Gayle and Stassya's matching dresses

3. Student Days

Our adventures continued with the students, the classes, and outings right up until Christmas. Friendships were forming amongst the students and their host sisters and brothers. The American high school students all knew each other, as they had all attended the same school in California. The Russian students also all knew each other, so it didn't take long for the two individual shy, quiet groups to become one—noisy, talkative and always laughing.

Some of our afternoon activities were local ones and some were tours out of town.

One day, we invited a belly dancer to come and perform and talk about herself. The students had fun trying out her moves. Another day, Marilyn and I brought some loaned wedding dresses and some fancy hats. The girls tried on the dresses and hats, put on lots of eye makeup, and posed for pictures.

Our next venture involved Tom, the founder of CHI who brought his 50's black Cadillac convertible with whitewall tires and a big V8 engine to show the students. We took a group picture with all of us either in, on top of, or all around this wondrous car. The school was near a country road with no one around, so Tom took each and every student for a ride past fields of curious cows, tall golden grass, with a bright sun shining in a blue sky. For these young people from Leningrad, a big, bustling city deep in snow and ice this time of year, it must have been like a dream.

Sally, the belly dancer

Jane trying on wedding dress

Gayle, Marilyn, Stassya on left, and group

One of our full-day tour outings took us to San Francisco by way of the ferry. "Oohs and aahs" came from each student as we neared the city. The Golden Gate Bridge sparkled in the sunlight with a whisper of fog hanging over the very top. We rode the cable car from near the ferry terminal at Pier One to Fisherman's Wharf. We had a delicious lunch at Sabella's Restaurant and topped it with ice cream cones at Ghirardelli Chocolate Factory. Our bus picked us up near Pier 39 and I noticed twenty-five heads nodding off as we took the thirty-minute ride back across the Golden Gate Bridge to San Anselmo.

Another of our tour outings was to Sacramento. After our tour of the State Capitol building, several students asked if we could sit in on a session of the State Congress for a few minutes. We slipped quietly into seats in the back of the visitor's gallery and viewed what, to these students, may have been an eye-opening experience into how our democratic society works. Next came a visit to Sutter's Fort and after that we spent the rest of the day in Old Town. While we were there, Stassya and I posed for a picture, wearing old-fashioned gowns and hats from the Gold Rush Days.

The Gold Rush Girls

4. Christmas and Goodbye

Christmas Eve in our home is a time of family gathering around the Christmas tree. For Christmas of 1989, we had homemade turkey soup, warm bread, and lots of decorated cookies. You could smell the hot apple cider as soon as you came in the front door. There were enough family members so that we had to sit on the floor, on the stairs, and on any sofa or chair you could grab first. We gave Stassya the place of honor, in the middle of our white sofa facing the fireplace. There was a crackling fire. The mantle was covered with pine branches and candles which reflected in the mirror. The tree was decorated with many ornaments from other countries which I had collected on our travels. Stassya hung her antique looking, very delicate Russian glass ornaments on the tree. Presents wrapped in red, silver and gold sparkled under the Christmas lights. Everything was very festive, and we were all talking at once.

Finally, it was time to open our gifts. One family member was chosen to be Santa, and as most of the presents were for Stassya, they were stacked in front of her. Her eyes were wide, and she had a child-like smile as she peeled the tape back, first one end, then the other. She carefully unwrapped each gift and folded the paper, smoothing out the wrinkles. She placed the bows all around her and snuggled right into our family. My whole family, my mother, sister, sons and daughter, and their spouses enjoyed meeting Stassya and sharing our family Christmas with her.

Three days after Christmas, it was time to take our new-found Russian friends to the airport and send them first to Disneyland and then home to their families in Leningrad. We sent them off with lots of hugs and tears, and a lot more luggage than they had come with. We were sure we would never see each other again, so Stassya and I both wore our matching dresses to the airport and clung to each other

23

until the last moment.

We knew our countries were not friendly, and that it would be most difficult to keep in touch. We were crying and laughing at the same time. We knew we had found a lasting friendship despite our language, history, and cultural differences. But we had to say good-bye, and it would most likely be forever. Stassya promised to write as soon as she returned to Leningrad.

A tearful goodbye

5. Letters from Leningrad

Stassya's precious letter from Washington, DC (see page 12) had arrived so quickly, but after that I received nothing!

Why am I not hearing from her? Is she getting my letters? What is wrong with the mail service? Are her promised letters swimming across the sea? These questions haunted me and I ran out to the mailbox every day looking for a letter from Stassya.

Stassya had filled our house so completely for three weeks with her personality, her stories, her childlike wonder, and then, suddenly, she was gone. Our home felt empty. I felt bereft and lonely. I had a new friend and couldn't see her or talk to her or go out to lunch and gossip with her which made her letters all the more precious to me.

Where were they? And was she okay?

Early in January, Tom and Lilka had a reunion party for the host families in their home. The families came to share experiences, pictures, stories, and some tears. During the party, Tom stood up and waited for everyone to quiet down.

"I have an announcement to make," Tom then declared loudly. With a broad smile on his face, Tom said,

"I have completed arrangements with Mr. Korevsky to send a group to Leningrad (later to be renamed St. Petersburg) this summer for a homestay. The families in Leningrad are excited to be hosts for the American students who had hosted their family members. I have asked Gayle to put the trip together and accompany them along with her husband Jim." Tom's head swiveled as he looked around the room, "and Jim," he went on, "I would like you to record the trip with both photos and video for our archives." I smiled with delight and anticipation. Everyone clapped, and in no time I had a list of prospective students and CHI staff members eager to participate.

In February, I finally received a letter dated early in January.

~ ☕ ~

[From Leningrad:]

January 8, 1990
My dear Gayle and Jim!
I have returned home and become a sort of Santa Claus putting the presents under the fir trees of my relatives and friends. [Christmas is celebrated on January 7th in Russia according to the Russian Orthodox Church.] *Helen was the happiest one she got more presents than other people and loved her new stuffed fox very much. They are sitting at the table together and she gives him the most tasty pieces. At night they sleep together and Helen read him fairy-tales to sleep well. I think Fred the Fox will be able to speak by August.*

Paul is very happy that I am at home. He missed me badly. He doesn't like the idea of my going away (But I can't live without going to different places.) Now he is so happy, kind and tender, it looks like honey-moon. I began to fulfil my revolutionary plans to change woman's position in the house. After the parting he slaves joyfully. I hope that it will last for a long time.

I am looking for August. Paul is very enthusiastic about your coming and we began to discuss plans (I want to be ready with my choices). It is very nice to dream about summer, but it is winter and rather cold one. Today is -15 degrees Celsius. We are going to skate. We wear fur hats coats, boots. It is funny to put on all warm things. In them we look very stout even my slender Helen. But it helps to keep warm. No green hills, no beautiful flowers. White, gray and black are the colours of winter. I am very glad that you had chance to see winter in Europe. I'll be happy to know your impressions after your trip. I hope it was very interesting.

I'll be waiting for your letters.
Kiss you, miss you. Yours, Stanislava.

26

Helen's (age 9) drawing of a Russian woman

I love it. I love it! I thought. Paul [her husband] *slaves joyfully, and Stassya is going to be the revolutionary woman, changing the role of women in Russia! I love it! Good luck, my funny friend.*

Her letter made me laugh as we had for those three memorable weeks. I was glad to know that she missed us, too, and was waiting for my letters. But then I reread Stassya's letter. Her use of the words *slaving* and *revolutionary* now jumped out at me and had me worried. *Is someone reading our letters?* A year later I would ask myself that same question. Stassya's next letter would not arrive until late in March.

[From Leningrad:]

February 20, 1990
My Dear, wonderful Gayle!
You even can't imagine how precious and special your help is. Your wonderful letters written on the 2nd and the 8th are the best

27

medicine for me. I got them on the 16th of February. They helped me to recover, returned me to happy memories. They forced me to sit down and write to you.

At the end of January I suffered the greatest lost. My father was paralyzed after a stroke and after three days in hospital he died in my arms. It was so terrible. From the very morning of the 25th of January when he had the second stroke, nothing could be done. He didn't feel anything, didn't react only his heart was beating and blood was going out of his mouth. The heart was weaker and weaker…he died at 20 minutes to 4 p.m. We buried him at the old cemetery on the 30th of January. I could hardly move, think. I tried to spend all my time with mother. It was a hard and unexpected blow to her. They have been married since 1950. Helen was at my neighbour's. I went to the cemetery every other day. In a week I began working at school, it was rather difficult. Everything was black and grey the weather was gloomy, nasty, no sun, no blue sky. I was doing all the necessary things because I was used to do it but I had to take some medicine to recover. And suddenly I got 2 wonderful, kind, clever charming letters from you. Two cute cranes [I had learned some origami, the art of paper-folding, from some of my Japanese students and included the two cranes in my previous letter.] *helped me to look at the sky and to see the light. Wonderful memories and sweet hopes have helped me to overcome my pain.*

I am waiting for you in August. Kiss Jim and best wishes to all members of your family. You have given me strength. Thank you, darling. Best wishes from Paul and Helen. Yours, Stassya

After I read Stassya's letter, I cried. I wanted to let her cry on my shoulder and to comfort her. I remembered finding out, upon arriving home from a trip that my father had passed away while I had been gone. When I had left on my trip that day in June of 1985 to escort a group of high school girls to Japan, I had no inkling it was the last time I would see my father. My last image of him was at the front of the restaurant where he and my mother had taken Jim and me for breakfast before I left for the airport. He was his usual fun self, but then poignantly took off his good-luck pin, a small green horseshoe, and handed it to me. We had just been discussing the perils of traveling with young teenaged girls, with their high energy, their constant chattering, and their unexpected exploits.

"To keep you safe," he said, and then added with a big smile, "and sane."

How was I to know that he would need that pin more than me when he collapsed with a heart attack in a local bank three weeks later. While on my trip, I had no communication with my family at home. However, while flying home on the airplane, I had been hit with a deep melancholy, which I didn't understand at the time, and which prompted some of the girls to ask me if I was all right.

"I don't know," I had told them. "I'm okay, maybe just tired and let down after all the excitement."

Jim and our daughter Joelle had met me at the San Francisco airport. I appreciated their enthusiasm in welcoming me home and wanting to know about my trip. I regaled them with my stories. When we finally arrived home, I went straight to bed.

Just as soon as I had begun to relax, Jim came into the bedroom, and sat down on the bed. He took my hand and with tears in his eyes, said,

"I have some very bad news to tell you, and I knew you would not want me to wait."

Sensing his reluctance, with my heart beating like a drum, I immediately sat back up. He took me in his arms and said in a soft voice which was breaking up as he held back tears,

"Your father had a heart attack, he passed away late yesterday."

I pulled back and looked at him in disbelief. I reminded Jim that my father had been fine when I left three weeks earlier. But somehow I knew it was true, and knew why I had suddenly been overcome by a sense of dread on the airplane. I had to go to my mother and asked Jim to drive me to my mother's apartment.

Grief and funeral planning took the place of the usual overwhelming jetlag that comes with returning to the United States from Japan.

Now, upon receiving my dear friend's letter, I understood what she was going through. But then sadness for Stassya's loss and the bittersweet memory of my father were replaced by gladness that my last two letters to my friend had helped her regain her life. August couldn't come soon enough.

Stassya's next letter arrived in late May.

~ ~

[From Leningrad:]

April 8, 1990
Dear Gayle and Jim,

Today we have a real holiday. We have got a small package with your wonderful pictures about your trip to Europe and very poetic charming, long, interesting letter. Gayle, darling, you are very good at writing. I enjoyed the letter even more than famous "Gone with the Wind." I am very proud to be your personal translater. Every time I read your letter I improve my translation but still it is too far from the beauty of the original. Your letters (and my ones too) have to do a very hard work to "walk" through the country to swim like a dog across the Atlantic Ocean. That is why it takes about 5-6 weeks to reach the addressee. But after a long waiting the joy of getting it very great. The news that you are coming together with Jim is very great. I am looking forward. We have ordered already many excursions about Leningrad museums. We are doing our best to organize trip to Moscow and Novgorod, Pushkin and Pavlosk. We have many interesting ideas so I don't think that an extra day-off will be possible.

I am waiting for the list of American students. It'll be so nice to see our American host mothers and students we met in America. It's a pity that some of them are starting their college in August. Maybe next time another month would be better. I hope to hear your voice but I realize that it is very difficult to go through. In Leningrad they take several orders for calls to America (which can be done in several days) at 10 a.m. I do teaching at this time. I used to dial the number at our teacher's room but all my attempts were in vain.

You know, Gayle, I speak to you almost every day. I try to see everything with your eyes trying to explain you things, ideas, events. I am putting into my table all interesting articles from the newspaper "Moscow News" which is published in English for you to read in August.

I am very happy that you enjoyed your trip and didn't get cold in the snows of Europe. Did you play snowballs? Thank you for wonderful pictures. I never saw Mozart's House and German beer pubs with musians and a puppet man is so nice. You both look so nice, young and happy. Your descriptions of Vienna were so picturesque that I could visualize the beauty of that world famous place. I even could imagine you standing in the middle of old square listening to accordion.

I hope you'll like my beautiful city. It is unique and it doesn't have anything like in America. Russian style in everything.

You have written that you had a lot to do after your trip. I can close my eyes and see your wonderful stairs filled with papers. Now I understand why I fail to do all my work. I need stairs to devide all the amount of work into small portions on step for each time.

Everything is piled on me and I can't do anything. The idea of Paul and Helen helping me is very sweet but I was to kind-hearted to start the revolution at home. Cooking takes two-three hours every day. Then washing, cleaning. I am tired of thanking my poor hands.

On Mondays I go to the Teacher's Institute to improve my teaching methods and English. On the weekdays I have 7 lessons with students dayly, then English with Helen and Paul plus home duties and tire-out mother begins to get ready for the next day lessons at school. And after midnight I have some time to enjoy TV or reading but I am to sleepy for that. Weekend planned beforehand flies very quickly. I spent it at my mother's place helping her about the house and we go to the father's grave every Sunday.

But in spite of that I try to know all the latest events in policy. We live in a very interesting period. Changes are so great and sometimes unexpected. But I hope that everything will be all right. People must understand that we have many other vital problems to solve. Peace is the most wonderful task for all of us.

I often remember our wonderful Christmas day when we played all together. Thank you for very special impressions. I love and miss you so badly. I am waiting for August.

Yours, Stanislava

~ 🍵 ~

I had not realized that my filing method was so noticeable. The bottom step is used for things to take in the car for errands, the next step up is used for things that must go upstairs to my office. The third step is for things that must go upstairs for putting away in the closet. Then it is all repeated upstairs, with things that must go down. It is probably best that Stassya doesn't have stairs.

In the hopes of having our letters and packets pass back and forth more quickly, we soon developed a system to send letters with friends and colleagues who were traveling abroad. Some letters were hand-carried to and from Russia and some arrived from England and some from Sweden. The next letter arrived from Sweden containing our unofficial official invitation.

I couldn't wait to see Stassya again and to meet Stassya's husband Paul and daughter Helen. I also wanted to get to know my new friend better. The three weeks she had been in my home were fun and informative about her country. We had become fast friends, and I wanted to see the country she loved. But, I had been naïve and had visualized her living conditions much the same as ours. The realities came later and shocked me to the core.

Our invitation: "You are invited."

6. Welcome to Russia!

In preparation for our group's trip to the Union of Soviet Socialist Republics (USSR), passports and visas had to be obtained. That meant a trip to the Russian Consulate in San Francisco. Jim and I drove up to a white, clapboard Victorian house on a quiet street lined with large, leafy trees. At first glance, it looked innocent enough, although there was a white van parked just across and down from that spot. As we looked over our shoulders, I said to Jim under my breath, "Do you suppose we are being watched by the FBI?"

"No, that's only in Bond movies," he whispered.

We climbed the steep wooden stairs to the sturdy, windowless front door. To our surprise, it was locked. A small sign said, *Wait for the buzzer.* When the buzzer went off, we opened the door into a small waiting room. It was crowded with people, mostly speaking Russian. A few were seated, but most were standing in a long line that stretched right up to the door where we had entered. We stood where we were and waited patiently for our turn.

As we finally stepped up to the small, double-paned window, I saw her face. The expression was very stern, her lips in a straight line. Her hair was pulled severely back into a tight knot. She gave a quick impatient wave of her hand to indicate that I was to slide my paperwork into the slot under the window. No greeting was forthcoming. She looked over our paperwork very carefully, said something in a very curt voice, and waved her hand once again as if to brush us away. She pushed our paperwork back to us through the slot and in a loud, forceful voice, said, "Next!"

We then tucked tail, hung our heads, and crept slowly out the door carrying our papers—no visa, no nothing! Feeling like two naughty children who were scolded but didn't quite know what for, we descended the stairs to the sidewalk below and we looked at each other in confusion and dismay.

"What was that?" Jim said with a puzzled look on his face. "Did we do something wrong?"

I shrugged my shoulders as we proceeded to walk to our car, thinking, *Now what?*

Then I stopped, squared my shoulders, stuck out my chin, and said, "Damn it, we're Americans. We need to just march right back in there and find out what we need to do to get those visas!"

So back we went, up the stairs again, waited to get buzzed back in, and got in line (which was just as long as the first time). I did notice a couple of very slight smiles coming from some who were still seated. I acknowledged them with a nod and a slight smile of my own.

Again, we were given an abrupt hand motion indicating that we were to step to the window. I leaned down to be sure our stern lady could hear me through the thick window and asked her what we needed for our visas. I slipped the papers through the slot. She looked them over as if it were the first time, very carefully, stamped them, and said in a gruff voice, "The visas will be in the mail. Next..." We walked out with our heads held high, glanced over at the white van still parked across the street, and danced a little jig before getting into the car. I resisted the impulse to wave, but, I could almost hear applause coming from that suspicious van. Perhaps I imagined it?

We had passed our first, but not our last, hurdle with the formidable Russian bureaucracy. The group had grown to eighteen students and eight adults. A few weeks later, in August, we all left together out of San Francisco and flew directly to Helsinki, Finland. We stayed overnight, and flew on to Leningrad the next day. Now, I had a problem: how to smuggle hundreds of dollars into Russia.

In 1990 there was no way to send dollars to Russia to pay for our expenses. It was almost impossible to even correspond. Telephones were cut off in mid-conversation, letters took weeks, if they arrived at all. This was before the common use of computers and faxes. We did not want the school or families to pay for our buses, entrance fees, or food in restaurants, not to mention our overnight train to Moscow, hotel, and excursions there. Somehow, I had to take cash into Leningrad and lots of it, and hope Stassya would be able to exchange dollars for rubles.

I was afraid that a large amount of cash would be considered smuggling and would be confiscated, if found. After all, if caught, I imagined I could be jailed, tortured, used as an example, or held for ransom! With determination, I hid the cash on my body, zipped closed inside of pockets, worn in a money belt on my waist under my clothes, tucked into my bra, and even folded into my socks.

As I approached the customs agents, my heart was thumping, my hands sweating. Standing nearby were guards in their uniforms. They had guns and were holding the leashes of dogs sitting patiently waiting for instructions from their masters. As I got closer, my stomach churned in fear and guilt. I was afraid if I looked the custom agent in the eyes, I would give myself away. I was shaking so hard, tears threatened. I swallowed, took a deep breath, and timidly stepped up to the window, hoping I was not rustling with all that money hidden on my body. The stern face behind the glass looked me over as he took his time comparing my passport picture with the real me. I nearly fainted. He stamped my passport with what sounded like a gun shot and roughly signaled me to proceed. My legs were like jelly as I still expected to be stopped by a suspicious armed guard when I stepped across the line into our Cold War, enemy country.

All my fear going through customs was soon forgotten with the utter joy of seeing my friend standing and waiting for me at the airport in Leningrad. We were each wearing our matching, long-sleeved, black and white dresses. I planted my feet on Russian soil, and now I was the one with wide eyes, looking with wonder and curiosity. I also sometimes had painful and guilty feelings with even a bit of fear when I began to look more closely at my surroundings. But that came later after the excitement had ebbed a bit.

We were met by the host families at High School #160 and, after introductions, and instructions, and some apprehension, we parted ways knowing we would meet again the next day. Since we had luggage, Stassya had made arrangements for our daughter Joelle's host family to drive us to their apartment, instead of taking the bus as we did from then on. We drove out of the main part of the city and into the suburbs.

There were no trees, no flowers, and no grass. Dozens of identical concrete buildings stood at angles to each other, each several stories high. Stassya's apartment was on the fifth floor. As we entered her building, the small concrete entry was very dim. As she held the metal door for us, we squeezed onto a very small elevator that smelled strongly of urine. We pressed in close as it lumbered up the five floors. We exited onto a dim and dingy hallway and came to a thick, heavy door.

Stassya opened the door with her key, stepped inside, and turned on the light. Jim and I were pleasantly surprised by the cheerful entry with colorful flocked wallpaper, and a chest-high bookcase with a telephone sitting on a snow-white, crocheted doily given to Stassya by my mother when Stassya was visiting us in California. Immediately in front of us was a tiny little kitchen with a wooden table and chairs. The curtains on the window were white and sheer. You could look straight out to another such building and down to the gravelly dirt-lined sidewalk. The walls were covered in cheerful blue and white patterned wallpaper. There was a small stove with a bright red teapot sitting on a burner. Next to the stove, sitting majestically on the counter, was a Russian *samovar* (a colorfully decorated and uniquely shaped urn plugged in to keep water eternally hot for the next cup of tea). We used this to keep clean drinking water available. On another wall was a very small sink. Above the sink was a cabinet with only slats for a bottom. There the dishes were stacked in a holder to drip dry over the sink after being washed.

Stassya led us down the hallway to the first room on our right. There was a small upright piano, lots of built-in storage cabinets which included a miniature desk area decorated with cute drawings, and a single bed. This was Helen's room. Next we were led to the end of the hallway into the living room complete with a comfy-looking sofa, a small TV, and a beautiful dark-wood cabinet with glass doors. In there were Stassya's treasures and books. There were blue patterned cups and saucers, teapots, and Russian porcelain eggs. The hand-painted enameled wooden boxes caught my eye. The pictures on them depicted scenes of Russian fairy tales. This was Stassya and Paul's bedroom as well as their living room. The sofa made into a bed at night. This was to be our room so we settled in.

I began to wonder when we would meet Stassya's family, but that was not to be for a few days, as her husband Paul and nine-year-old daughter Helen were staying in the country at their *dacha* so that we could use Stassya and Paul's bedroom, and Stassya could sleep in Helen's room. Stassya's father had built the *dacha* (a little wooden house on a small piece of land out in the countryside). After WWII her father along with seventy-five co-workers, had petitioned the government for some land. They were given use of a swampy wetland surrounded by forest. He and Stassya's mother Sophia would go out in the evening and pick through the wooden boxes which had been thrown out behind the local store. They pulled the boxes apart, stacked the wooden slats, and then carried them three or four miles back to their piece of land. He used what materials he could find with whatever simple tools he'd had at hand. Sophia had planted a garden there. Stassya and her sister Nina helped in the garden during the summers as they were growing up. This was and still is a common way for the people of Leningrad to have a country home during the summer and also to be able to provide fresh food for their families. They canned and bottled what they could for the winter months when fresh food was not so abundant due to the extreme cold weather. Since this community was made up of fellow workers, everyone knew each other and looked forward to spending their summer weekends together. The children could run and play in the forest and swim in the small river nearby without their parents worrying about them. Everyone enjoyed the balmy "White Nights" of summer.

7. Our New Family

Finally, Paul and Helen showed up. It was Sunday and we spent the day together wandering the gardens of Pushkin. It was difficult speaking with Paul, as Stassya had to interpret back and forth between us, leaving the conversation stilted, with comments on the weather and the beautiful grounds. There was some laughter, as we watched the antics of Helen. At the end of our fun day together, Paul and Helen returned to the *dacha* and we to the apartment.

Helen drinking from the swan fountain

On the following Sunday, after Paul and Helen had arrived, we took a bus to the Russian forest on the outskirts of Leningrad. On our walk to the bus, Helen playfully tossed dried seed pods, with spines sticking out, onto the back of my sweater. Unbeknownst to me, several burrs had stuck, making me look like a porcupine. Jim, Paul, and Stassya were laughing, so I turned to see what was so funny. Helen threw one more onto my sleeve, and then I realized the joke was on me. I pulled it off and threw it back on Helen. She ducked and threw another. That sealed our bond right then. I fell in love with this little wraith of a child. She was thin and pale with a pert little nose. Her thin, short, and straight blond hair was pulled back in little pony tails, wrapped in colorful stretch bands. They wiggled as she skipped along, ahead of us now.

We entered the dark forest which reminded me of the Russian fairy tales Stassya had told us about in the evenings at the dining table in our home in Santa Rosa. The trees were thick and close together. The sun showed through in a few places like an arrow piercing the darkness. One such finger of light pointed to a beautiful, but sinister-appearing, large, red mushroom at the base of one of the leafy trees. We thought it was very unique until Stassya told us not to touch it because it was one of the most poisonous of all the mushrooms. Jim took a picture of it. We later framed it and hung it in our home where it remains to this day.

The Red Mushroom

On our third Sunday, as a family outing, we attended a Russian ballet, *Swan Lake*. It was my very first ballet, not Helen's. Stassya had told us the story on the way to the theater so we could follow it. Helen sat next to me, tipped forward on the edge of the seat so as not to miss a thing. I could tell that she was completely into the music and knew every note as her head was bobbing and swaying to the music. After the performance, I told Stassya that I would never go to another *Swan Lake* ballet performance, as I had seen the best there was in the country of its birth.

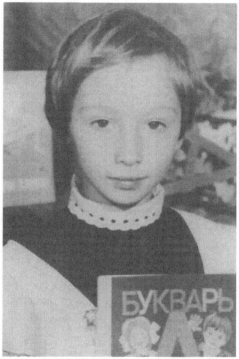

Helen, age 8

8. Sights of Leningrad

Our Welcoming Party was held in a former Palace which is now used for large meetings or events. The long room had elegant glass chandeliers, walls in white and gold, and tall, narrow windows trimmed in heavy velvet drapes held back by thick, tasseled ropes. There were long tables set up with food and soft drinks. The chairs were covered in velvet. That set the tone for the formal greetings and introductions. Stassya was the MC for the event. There were speeches given by the principal, Mr. Korevsky and myself as the leader of our group. An opera singer entertained us, and to finish off the festivities, each American student had to give a short introduction of him or herself in Russian. Stassya had helped us practice in our class the day before, but we all stumbled through with embarrassed grins and flushed cheeks.

After the formalities, everyone relaxed. There was lots of laughter, talking, and the clinking of glasses followed by *Nazdorovie* (the Russians have many toasts for different occasions. This one is not exactly the equivalent of "Cheers" but thanks the hosts). By the end of the evening it seemed that we had always been friends.

Meanwhile, during the weekdays and on Saturdays, Stassya had all the group members meet in her classroom at High School #160. She had fixed up her classroom to be very welcoming with soft, white curtains on the windows, and large, blue paper-flower decorations on the back wall. The student desks were in rows, with the teacher's desk up in the front. There was an upright piano near the door with blackboards on the remaining two walls. Stassya told me she had decorated it herself. It was light and cheerful, a nice contrast to the concrete buildings outside the window.

Stassya gave us a lesson each morning in her classroom about history or art, touching on what we were to see that day. During one session she was talking about World War II from her knowledge and viewpoint of Russian history. I realized that some of what she said about America's participation, or lack thereof, was not what I remembered being taught. It surprised me that Joshua, one of the high school boys knowledgeable of that period of American history, did not call her attention to the Lend/Lease program begun by President Franklin Roosevelt in 1941 meant to help our allies (first Great Britain) before we entered World War II ourselves. In 1942, the program of sending airplanes, tanks, ammunition, food rations, and other goods to support the Russian troops now our allies bogged down fighting the Nazis, started by sending ships to Murmansk a far northern port in Russia. This program lasted until the end of the war, and is considered by many historians to be a critical program for winning the war. Apparently, this information had been kept from the Russian people until after *Glasnost* in 1990.

During the break, I asked Joshua why he hadn't raised his hand to say something about the Lend/Lease program after Stassya commented that America wanted Russia to lose the war and, therefore, did not come to their aid. We were very informal in class so there was nothing intimidating holding him back.

"Mrs. Peebles," he said with heartfelt sincerity, "I would not hurt Stassya's feelings for anything."

"You're right, Josh," I said. "I see what you mean."

Our very first group tour led by Stassya in Leningrad was to the large cemetery within the city where over a million men, women, and children killed in Leningrad during the two year Nazi siege of World War II were buried in unmarked graves dug in long rows, one after another. Commemorative plaques were placed at the end of each row. It was a sobering experience, and later after meeting Stassya's mother Sophia, and hearing about her personal wartime experiences, it became real and personal. I tried to imagine what it must have been like, but it was beyond comprehension.

On the same day, we walked through the gardens of a small museum in Leningrad. Many of the city's statues and art treasures had been buried there during World War II to keep them from falling into the hands of the Nazis.

Stassya tried to make sure we saw each and every point of interest in and around Leningrad. During our visit to the Hermitage, I was amazed at the participation of all the high school students. There was no hanging back and chatting, there were no giggles, and no complaints to be looking at art work for at least two hours straight. We were all crowded closely around Stassya so as not to miss any details, as she told stories of each of her favorite pieces of art.

Stassya had been a docent at the Hermitage for some time and so was very familiar with the layout of this immense museum and palace of art. We climbed the opulent marble staircase with blue walls outlined in shiny gold. We viewed the Egyptian Room filled with sarcophagi containing mummies and valuable artifacts from the tombs. The Crown Jewels of Russia were in locked glass cases as were the priceless Faberge Eggs sparkling with diamonds, rubies, and emeralds which were designed for Romanov Czar Nicholas II's collection.

Another day, with our felt shoe coverings on, making us look like large walking mops, we were waiting in a long line in Catherine the Great's Palace to begin our tour. Stassya was doing her usual intense introduction to what we were to see and all the dramatic history surrounding Catherine the Great. I heard some whispering behind me coming from a group of the boys. I turned to see what it was all about. They were pointing excitedly, indicating a woman standing in front of and a little to the side of Stassya.

She was tall and slender, wearing a large orange hat decorated with blue ribbon trim, listening intently to every word from Stassya. She saw me looking at her and smiled. When the line started to move, she came over to me and asked if she could join our group so that she could hear what our tour guide was saying. She explained that her guide, a nice lady, spoke a little English, but was really more fluent in French.

By that time, the boys had told me who this woman was. They

recognized her from her TV series, *The Bionic Woman*. Yes, it was Lindsay Wagner! She crowded close to Stassya as we all did and never left her side. By the end of the tour, Lindsay was very intrigued about Stassya and was asking me questions about her. I explained who she was and what we were doing there, and that we were staying in Stassya's apartment. Lindsay was curious about details of where Stassya lived and what her apartment looked like, so I quickly asked Stassya if it was okay to invite Lindsay and her husband for a visit later that evening. After I told Stassya that Lindsay was a TV star, she became nervous about showing off her little apartment. But she agreed, and I issued the invitation. I wrote down the address and directions, we set a time for the meeting in the evening, and then we went on our way.

Upon arriving back at the apartment, we all quickly went to work. Paul, Stassya's husband who was at home when we got there, made up the package of green Jell-O I had brought from home. Helen straightened her room, and we all pitched in to make our living/bedroom presentable. Because all the apartment buildings were in a row and looked exactly the same, Jim went downstairs after dinner to stand outside the door so Lindsay and her husband would see him as they pulled up in their chauffeured car.

I am sure that they were a little concerned about what they had gotten themselves into when they stepped into the dim entry that smelled strongly of urine. They seemed to relax, however, as soon as they entered Stassya and Paul's cheerful and immaculately clean apartment. Lindsay brought Stassya a signed copy of her published vegetarian cookbook. Stassya sat on the floor at Lindsay's feet as they chatted away.

Jim was talking to Lindsay's husband Stephen who was a movie producer. He told Jim he was in Leningrad seeking out locations for a movie. My head swiveled back and forth trying to listen to both conversations. After an hour, Paul came into the room with an interesting combination of green Jell-O and vanilla ice cream which Lindsay said was perfect for her vegetarian diet. The visit ended on a happy note with lots of noisy talking and laughter.

9. Palaces to Potatoes

"But, dahling," Stassya said as she was hanging my underwear on a clothesline stretched across her kitchen about eye level. (Earlier, I'd had a lesson on how to use the Russian washing machine, a time-consuming project as buttons had to be pushed for each cycle. There was no dryer.)

"They are works of art," she continued with a sly smile.

"Well, I never thought of that," I said as I looked at the new artwork now hanging in her kitchen—a zebra print, two white dainties, and a silky black piece trimmed in black lace. We collapsed laughing and had a cup of tea.

The next day I understood what she meant when we were walking down Nevsky Prospect, the main shopping street in Leningrad. We stopped to look in a shop window, and Stassya pointed out one plain white, very large pair of cotton underpants hanging in the window. I also peeked inside the shop next door and saw only three pairs of shoes on display in the shop and nothing in that window.

After the opulence of the palaces of the day before, and even the subways decorated with marble pillars and colorful tile frescos on the walls, the dire lack of food choices and goods started to become even more heartbreaking. It was common to see someone parked on the street with the trunk of their car opened for only a moment to expose one dead whole chicken or a couple of potatoes for sale.

My visit to Stassya's local grocery store was as incredible to me as the supermarket where I lived had been to Stassya. We stepped inside a large, dimly lit building. The floor was gritty, the shelves mostly empty. Stassya stopped at the doorway and took inventory.

"There is no bread, no meat, no cheese, no fruit," she said in a quiet voice to herself. She quickly took out the jar she had brought with her and had the girl behind the counter fill it with yogurt. I strolled around the market aisles. I saw a few cans and some bags of what looked like dried beans but couldn't read the labels as they were in Russian.

I noticed a sound coming from the rear of the store, like a hiss. I kept walking and stumbled on what looked like a fight among some women. There was a lot of noisy activity there where I could see a bin with a few fish. Clearly there was not enough to go around. I hurried back down the aisle so as not to appear like I was snooping, and then walked slowly out of the store. Stassya paid for her small purchase, and joined me. I must have had a look of shock on my face.

"Now you have seen our situation," she said quietly.

I reached for her hand with tears in my eyes. I knew that she was proud of her country, the art, the history, the music, and the beautiful palaces. I smiled and squeezed her hand and, arm in arm we got on the streetcar and headed back to her apartment.

At the beginning of our stay in Leningrad, I was asked by Stassya not to speak English in public, which I didn't, not even in the hallway of her apartment building, but I could feel the looks and hear the whispers. My clothes and body language probably gave me away.

10. The Visit

Not long after that trip to the market, Stassya received a dinner invitation for us from the Berson family. About a year before, Joshua had hosted Sasha Berson, the oldest Berson son, in his family's opulent home in the hills of Tiburon overlooking the Golden Gate Bridge, so the next evening, Sasha Berson's family—mother, father, grandmother, and Yvgeny (Jenia), the younger brother of Sasha—were excited when they opened the door to greet us, and welcomed us with great enthusiasm.

During our visit in Sasha's home, Jim had fun videotaping all of us. Grandmother giggled with disbelief when she saw herself speaking and waving to the camera when Jim replayed the videotape for her. Sasha, the only family member who could speak English, stood up at the table before we started our meal, and thanked us for coming.

"When I left for America last December," he said, his voice cracking a little and emotion in his face. "I was not going to be influenced by anything you would show me. I was convinced that Russia was the greatest country in the world, that we were the happiest people and the kindest people, and that we had everything we needed." There were tears in his eyes and in mine as I recalled what we had seen and done during his visit to Marin County.

"As hard as it was, I have had to change my mind," he went on. "My experience in your country with my host family, and with the many generous and kind people I met, the grocery stores full of beautiful displays of fresh fruit and vegetables and plenty of meat, was a life-changing experience." He looked over at his mother who was signaling that she wanted to say something. Sasha began to interpret for her.

"Thank you for taking care of my son while he was in America," she said. "We are so grateful. Sasha has told us so much about your country, but soon he will be the age to be inducted into the military. For a Jewish boy, it could be a tragedy. There are stories of them being beaten and even raped," she said with tears running down her face. She waited for Sasha and then continued, "Would it be possible for you to sponsor him to go to America?" She then wiped her eyes with her apron, became the hostess once more, and began to serve our meal.

As thoughts circled in my mind, we ate at least three salads, two main dishes, and delicious black bread, accompanied by lots of vodka, laughter, and talk among seemingly old friends. As we said good-bye at the door, I leaned toward Sasha's mother.

"I'll find out how to sponsor your son," I whispered. "If it's at all possible, I'll do it." I could tell by the look in her eyes she understood what I had said.

A week later, we were invited to another host family apartment. When the family's four-year-old son opened a long, low cabinet in the living room, I saw stacks and stacks of green bananas piled inside. My first thought was, *what do you do with all those when they all ripen at once?* I usually bought three at a time, but if I stood in line for an hour or more to get them, I would probably feel pressured to buy a whole box of them. My daughter Joelle told me those bananas would be used to trade for something else, which explained my seeing food being sold out of the trunks of cars and the hoarding of items that could be used for trading.

The startling contrasts between Marin County, California, and Leningrad, Russia, started to weigh heavily on my mind. I found myself clinging to my friend as our departure drew near. There was not much time for me to reflect on this, however, as the students were having such a good time. They exuded laughter, curiosity, and thoughtfulness all at once; nevertheless I could see a change coming over them as well. It was evident in the questions they were asking and the whispered comments I overheard.

One evening, while sitting in Stassya's kitchen, Jim, Stassya, and I began some serious talking regarding the current politics and conditions we had witnessed in the everyday life of the Russian families living in Leningrad. Stassya shushed us, got up to close the glass-paneled doors of the kitchen, and sat back down.

"Please keep your voices low as we talk," she whispered. "I am absolutely sure my telephone is bugged by the KGB (Russia's secret police) because I am an English teacher, and have spent time in both England and America." She spoke so quietly that I had to lean in to hear her. I gulped as I realized that we could be placing Stassya and her family in jeopardy if Russia closed down once again to the rest of the world.

From that point, my visit was no longer a friendly, happy-go-lucky, laughter-filled visit with a friend. I became concerned and frightened for my friend, and worried about little Helen's health and future; she seemed so thin and pale. I was now more aware of what was around me, and was more sedate and thoughtful. I began to notice Stassya's darting eyes as we walked the streets and took public transportation. I also noticed how she puffed up and looked larger, somewhat like a mother hen might do to protect her brood, when she encountered any of the stern-looking matrons who were in charge of watching the visitors as they filed from room to room throughout the numerous palaces and museums we visited.

I was beginning to have the same feeling of being intimidated as I'd had at the Russian Consulate in San Francisco. I did not like the feeling. When I saw a line of Russian tanks driving down one of the main streets in Leningrad, I began to look forward to going home. And, I wanted to wrap my friend in my arms and take her with me.

11. An Unexpected Visit

One day we discovered that Stassya's apartment had no hot water. According to her, this happens periodically in Leningrad with no warning. She had hoped we would not be affected during our visit. Stassya telephoned her mother Sophia, who, being on the other side of Leningrad and not having had her hot water turned off, generously offered to have us come and use her apartment shower, and even offered to include dinner. So, later we went out to get a taxi.

In order for Stassya to negotiate the fare without the taxi driver thinking that he had rich foreigners at hand, she asked us to wait around the corner, and not to speak at any time during the ride. We obeyed, and when she had settled on the price, she motioned us to get into the car. We soon made the trip across the city to Sophia's apartment, where we were warmly greeted in Russian by a lively *babushka*. She had towels for our shower laid out for us and her table set with her best Russian dishes. We had a sumptuous meal of pork and roasted potatoes, and then finished with a meringue cake. Stassya told us there was no flour, so her mother made the dessert with egg whites. It looked like a Pavlova with a large divot in the middle. (This is a dessert that was concocted in either New Zealand or Australia—they each claim this—to commemorate the world tour of the famous Russian ballerina Anna Pavlova in the 1920s). But instead of the usual fruit (such as kiwi or bananas) and whipped cream filling, the divot was filled with fresh flowers as a decoration. The cake was delicious, and the flowers were wrapped and given to us to take back to Stassya's apartment. We thanked Sophia for our hot showers and lovely dinner. After we arrived back to Stassya's apartment, she told us part of her mother's story:

Sophia had been trapped in Leningrad with a baby, Stassya's older half-sister, during the World War II siege by the Nazis in September of 1941. The city suffered twenty-eight air raids on just one day alone—September 26th. Many of the places where food was stored went up in flames and burned for days. In one warehouse, the burlap bags that stored the sugar burned causing the sugar to run out and onto the street. Desperate people scooped it up even though it was mixed with dirt. It became a source of income for some.

The siege lasted for Nine Hundred Days, as to which this hellish period is commonly referred. In winter it was somewhat easier to get supplies, as Lake Ladoga outside of Leningrad was frozen over, and trucks could drive over it to deliver the precious food into the city. During the siege, the population decreased due to the deaths of an estimated one million people by starvation, and by the evacuation of thousands of the city's weak and elderly along the frozen truck route, which eased the strain on the remaining people. However, during the summer months, it was impossible to get supplies, while the Germans continued to ravage the city with gunfire and bombs. Some people went insane with hunger. There were corpses in the street with the death rate at first higher among the men. The people of Leningrad lived through hell with no heat in winter, frozen water pipes, virtually no food, and continual bombardment by air and heavy artillery attacks. The Russian people had wept for joy when the blockade was finally broken in January of 1944, almost three years later.

During the blockade, in order to qualify for a daily ration of one-quarter pound of bread, you had to work. Stassya's mother Sophia was hired to clean the vehicles which carried grain within the city to the mill for grinding. She was able to eat a meal of bread at work; therefore she could bring her allotted ration home for her baby and her own mother who also lived with her. The bread was only fifty percent flour, the rest consisting of sawdust and other unknown ingredients. At that time, Sophia had a very small metal stove with a chimney directed out a window. She would fry the pieces of bread and grind it to make a broth to feed her baby.

By 1946, Sophia had lost two husbands to the war, which ended in 1945. In 1950, Sophia was invited by her aunt, who still worked at the same mill, to attend a Christmas party at the mill factory. There she met the man who had hired her in 1943. He later became Sophia's husband of forty years, and was Stassya's father. During the siege, he had been in charge of destroying the factory in case the

Nazis invaded the city. He actually slept in the room which stored the dynamite!

During a tour of one Russian church, Stassya and I lit candles in remembrance of our two fathers. We could just picture them shaking their heads over our friendship after all those years of the Cold War, years of enmity, mistrust, and threats between our two countries.

12. Goodbye to New Friends

Our visit to Leningrad was coming to a close. First, we had a goodbye party to plan. At my suggestion, knowing the shortage of nearly everything we usually took for granted, all the members of our group had collected bits and pieces of unused or no longer needed items from our luggage and purses—such things as Q-tips, pens, notepads, gum, candies, post-it notes, small calculators, nail files, cologne, small packages of tissues, paperclips, and more. We separated them all out and used the items to fill decorated gift bags for each host family, with each student including a handwritten and illustrated thank-you note in their bag.

For the upcoming party, all of our students planned skits and songs, and the families brought desserts and tea. Stassya arranged for an accordionist, and I planned a little goodbye speech using my very limited Russian. On the day of the party, everyone enjoyed the evening of eating, laughter, skits and songs by the students, and the spontaneous and lively Russian dance by Stassya. The host sisters and mothers grabbed me and soon everyone joined Stassya in a raucous dance around the room, accompanied by the accordionist.

The highlight and end of the evening was topped by little Helen, who stood before us, very serious; and, in her sweet hesitant voice, she started to sing "My Bonnie Lies over the Ocean" in perfect English. She sang two verses, and when she began the last chorus, we all joined in. Helen looked over her shoulder at us in surprise, smiled, and continued singing without missing a beat. There wasn't a dry eye in the room.

On the day of leaving, tearful goodbyes and hugs were passed around on the train platform as we waited to board our overnight sleeper car. We stood with piles of luggage surrounding us, purses slung over shoulders, and a small carpet rolled up and carried by one of the boys who had purchased it as a gift for his family back home. As we pushed our way onto the train steps, slinging our heavy bags up to the top step, last-minute touches, goodbyes, and thank-yous sounded from everyone. As our train pulled away, we all crowded next to the windows on the platform side of the train car, waving and blowing kisses until we could no longer see our new friends in the distance.

Stassya and Ludmilla were accompanying us to Moscow. They took charge and assigned the sleeping compartments. There were four bunks in each compartment with a washroom and toilet at the end of the car. We heard a lot of chattering and laughter along the corridor, which later settled down to light singing and whispers. Jim grabbed one of the upper bunks in our compartment which was being shared with us three women, and promptly went to sleep. Stassya, Ludmilla, and I sat and talked quietly almost all night

13. Moscow

We arrived at the station in Moscow very early the next morning, where we were met by a bus and driver, and immediately taken to a hotel off Red Square. While checking in, we were asked for our passports which we were told would be held for us until we departed. That was a bit of a shock as I had instructed the students to give me their passports for safekeeping and here I was giving them all over to complete strangers in a hotel! When Stassya saw me about to object, she immediately cut in and said,

"That is the practice with foreigners in Russia. You have no choice."

"Well, that is that," I thought as I handed over our precious American passports.

Jim and I took our room keys and made our way to the third floor. Upon exiting the elevator, we encountered what seemed like the same stern matronly woman we'd seen in all the museums and palaces in Leningrad and at the San Francisco Russian Consulate. She was sitting at a small table facing the hallway. Not being sure of her role, I nodded and proceeded to our room. I opened the door to a sparsely furnished room with a regular-sized double bed with a metal headboard and footboard, a speckled brown linoleum floor, and a ceiling light. I looked around for some KGB bugs in the room. I was sure they were there, but they must have been hidden very well. (I heard later from a former Russian tour guide that I was right.) The bathroom had a toilet, a sink hanging on the wall, and a very small dark and grungy shower which made one of our cheapie motels look like the Ritz!

I don't remember the food in the public places where we ate nor the service, but I do remember the public toilet facilities. In one place, on an excursion trip rest stop out in the countryside, the smell emanating from a small outhouse was so bad that the girls and women all chose to go out into a field and use the bushes instead. We all laughed, calling out to each other, some of us soiling our shoes in the process! But these young people from Marin County never made a complaint or a sour face. They surprised me in so many ways. They absorbed, they participated, and they helped each other when needed, not only with heavy luggage, but with the inevitable culture shock that hits many people while being immersed in a foreign country. One young girl had a severe case of culture shock and homesickness causing her to be anti-social for some time before she snapped out of it. I later found out that when she went on to college, she majored in International Studies and went to Germany to study for a year.

By this time in my career with CHI, I had been put in charge of developing the Outbound Department and was also in charge of the incoming high school students from different countries who home-stayed in Sonoma and Napa Counties while attending school. This is the kind of impact I saw over and over during my work with students, both coming to the USA and our young people going to other countries to study. Parents would call to tell me how much their son or daughter had changed after their exchange homestay experience. The students had become more conscious of world affairs, interested in other people and cultures, and most became fluent in the language of the country they had stayed in for six months to a year. Others traveled and some went on to study for careers in international companies, overseas government offices, or teaching English in a school or company in Europe or Japan. All were impacted in some way, even after difficult beginnings with the local language, feelings of loneliness owing to homesickness and culture shock. It used to amaze me that even three weeks can make a difference in a young person's life choices.

Now on our first day in Moscow, we ventured out to Red Square and stood gawking at the colorful St. Basil Cathedral at one end, Gum Department Store near the side of the Cathedral, and across from Gum, the Kremlin, and, next to that, the building with Vladimir

Lenin's tomb inside. The monumental granite structure of the tomb reminded me of the ancient Step Pyramid in Egypt. We watched the changing of the guards at the tomb building. It was raining slightly so they did their goosestep march with raincoats on. When they switched guards, one took the raincoat off the other and placed it on the shoulders of the now outgoing guard. This was repeated again, and then the two replaced guards goose-stepped down the stairs, adjusted their raincoats in perfect unison so as to cover their guns from the dripping rain, and marched off, as the Kremlin bells finished the slow cadence signaling twelve noon. The loud, deep sound of those bells reverberated throughout the square and right through my body. They continued twelve times, lasting for the duration of the changing of the guards.

There was a very long line of people waiting to view Lenin in his sarcophagus. Everyone in our group wanted to get in line. I declined and stood with Stassya against the side of a building. Stassya had several of the students' cameras slung around her neck and, between us we held everyone's cameras which were forbidden inside the tomb. While standing there, we watched the comings and goings in and out of the Kremlin. Soon long, black limos with darkened windows began to dart quickly through the square, slowed to go through the large opening into the fortress, and then disappeared behind the closed gate. I wondered if I had glimpsed President Mikhail Gorbachev as he was driven by.

Stassya in Red Square

57

When the group came back together after their slow walk past Lenin's coffin, Stassya and I sorted and passed out the cameras. After that, we all went inside and walked through the Gum Department Store which is actually a shopping mall. It is a beautiful, airy building, painted white inside, with banners hanging from the high ceiling; it looked like a large greenhouse. There were three floors connected across the central open walkway by bridges with delicate hand-wrought iron railings. At close inspection, many of the shops were closed and empty, although there were crowds of people looking for merchandise and mingling around a large fountain in the middle of the central walkway on the first floor.

We did not see much of anything to buy in the way of souvenirs. My daughter Joelle later told me that she had gone into one of the open shops. She said the shop girls seemed reluctant to assist her as they continued their conversation while ignoring her. She looked around, did not see anything she wanted to purchase, and walked out. Then Stassya and Ludmilla took us to a "hard currency" shop for foreigners outside of the mall and around the corner where we could purchase traditional Russian items. We quickly snatched up items like painted, nested Matryoshka Dolls, jeweled Fabergé eggs, (copies, of course), hand-painted souvenir spoons, delicate old-fashioned Victorian-style Christmas tree decorations, and illustrated children's Russian fairy tale books to take home with us for ourselves and as gifts for family and friends. We were surprised to learn that Russians were not allowed to purchase anything in those shops!

Our bus tour of the city took us past the Bolshoi Theater and many government buildings, one of them which housed the original *Communist Manifesto by Karl Marx*. We stopped at the University of Moscow and exited the bus at an overlook of the city. The Moskva River flowed far below, winding through the city, was lined with trees beyond which we could see the low buildings of Moscow with an occasional colorful church dome reaching high above the surrounding buildings. While standing at the waist-high wall, Jim interviewed one of the students with the video camera turned on and asked him about his experiences.

"Patrick, what was your best memory of Leningrad?" Jim asked.

"It was the people," Patrick said with a wide smile, "definitely the host families. And the train ride to Moscow was amazing it was like stepping back in time. I was so excited, I couldn't sleep."

As he spoke, I noticed the large black circles under Patrick's eyes, making him look as though he had run into a very heavy door. He must have been exhausted, though pleasantly so.

We made a stop at one of the large squares in the central part of Moscow. During our walk through the square, a small ragged little boy of about four years old approached Jim. Stassya told Jim to ignore him and keep walking.

"He is a gypsy child," she said, "And has been taught to beg by his mother, over there, sitting against the building. Don't look at her. He is severely punished if he does not obey his mother."

Jim did as Stassya told him; however the little boy grabbed Jim's leg and held on as Jim kept walking. I could see he would rather have picked up that little ruffian and hugged him close. Then the boy finally let go, turned to Jim, and spit at him. Jim was speechless. I could tell the episode made him sad.

As we continued our city bus tour, we passed a familiar icon no one could ignore! There was a very large McDonald's sign on the side of one of the buildings we were passing.

"This is the first and only McDonald's restaurant in the USSR. It just opened a few days ago," our tour guide laughingly said.

There was a line that seemed to stretch to the horizon, four people across.

"Stop"! We all shouted at the same time, laughing and poking each other. "We want to eat lunch here!"

After eating unfamiliar Russian food for nearly three weeks, a hamburger and French fries sounded like manna and honey. We piled out of the bus and stood in line.

"You know what I like," Jim said to me. "Just make my order while I get some pictures and video of this incredible event we have stumbled on to."

One and a half hours later, the rest of us entered the large double doors. There was a very long counter with at least twenty registers with a clerk at each one taking orders and shouting them out in Russian. It was such an amazing sight that it took a moment for us to realize that we had to scatter and get in separate lines. I made my order for Jim and myself.

When it arrived, I went outside where there were dozens of tables, nearly all full. People were speaking Russian all around me. Finally I spied some chairs at a table where two of the adults in our group were already seated. I didn't see Jim waiting anywhere so I ate both orders—two hamburgers, two orders of fries, and two chocolate shakes—without regret!

59

Russian McDonald's brochure (1990)

When Jim showed up at my table and saw that I had eaten his McDonald's lunch, he was a good sport and just went over to interview one of the boys. It was Patrick again.

"What did you order?" Jim asked him.

"Well, I started with three hamburgers, two orders of fries, two cokes, a chocolate shake and finished with an apple pie!" The student said with a gleam in his eye. "It was worth the long wait," he added with a grin as he rubbed his full stomach.

When we returned to the bus, I could hear Jim's stomach growling, so I offered him a health food bar from my purse.

"You owe me," he grumbled as he downed the confection in three big bites.

Just as it began to get dark, we went out from our hotel to Red Square. It was about 11:00 pm. The cathedral was lit up and glowed red, green, and golden against the darkening sky. The large red star at the top of the Kremlin seemed to be blinking. We laughed and chatted with each other, turning around and around in order to see everything. It was a memorable and beautiful ending to our stay in Russia.

14. Welcome Home!

The next morning it was time to go home. As I stood at the checkout counter in the lobby of the hotel, I received back my stack of our groups' passports, much to my relief. I personally passed them out to each person to make sure we had all of them. Our bus was waiting for us near the hotel, and we boarded and settled in for the long ride to the airport. Stassya and I sat silently together with our hands locked in a vise grip. We still had a job to do; so, after sorting and claiming our luggage from the bus, we marched into the airport and lined up at check-in. That part went smoothly so off we went to the departure gate, still dragging our luggage.

I watched as each student said a tearful goodbye to Stassya and went through the turnstile barrier where we were to check our luggage before boarding the plane. I stayed behind to be sure everyone had gone into the open area beyond the barrier. Up until now, the logistics of getting each one in the group to this point had kept the tears back, but now they started to flow. This time I knew for sure I would never see Stassya again. I couldn't let go of her. We stood frozen to the spot.

"Sweetheart, we have to go," Jim said in a gentle voice, as he took my arm and guided me reluctantly through the turnstile.

Just beyond that barrier was the conveyor belt where we put our luggage. When it all disappeared, two uniformed guards confronted me. They spoke Russian in loud, staccato voices. They became very insistent. I was frightened and confused. I turned to Stassya who had heard the exchange from the other side of the barrier. She stormed through the turnstile, marched right up to the faces of the guards, and spoke very forcefully in Russian. She sounded like the stern Russian woman Jim and I had encountered at the Consulate in San Francisco! Whatever she said made the guards quickly back off. With a flick of their wrists, they motioned Jim and me to move on to the boarding gate.

"They wanted money for what they said is overweight luggage. Go, go, go," Stassya whispered in my ear, as I hugged her one more desperate time and turned to follow the group, some of whom looked back at me with worried frowns. I ran on ahead of them motioning for them to hurry and follow me.

We boarded our Aeroflot flight headed to Helsinki, Finland, and took our seats. The doors closed tightly immediately behind us and, to our amazement, we were the only ones on the flight! So much for concerns of overweight luggage....

As we rose into the sky over the city of Moscow and began our flight high above the countryside of Russia, I stared out the window, saying goodbye over and over. Tears were flowing freely now, and soon I was sobbing, thinking I had lost my friend forever.

When we descended into Finland, I had my hands over my ears. Apparently, Aeroflot airlines did not pressurize their airplanes and the pain from the pressure change was so great, I had to hold my breath and bite my tongue to keep from screaming. At last, Mother Earth wrapped us in her arms and set us down onto what felt like safe and familiar surroundings after what we had all just been through.

As our airplane came to an abrupt stop, all the empty seats flopped forward and down. We laughed until tears rolled down our faces. The relief of leaving Russia was overwhelming, even more so when we arrived at our beautiful hotel with sparkling white bathtubs and hot, running water. I immediately drew a bath, climbed into the warm tub, and lay soaking until the water became cool.

That evening, we all met in the lobby to go to dinner. On the way to the restaurant, we walked down the main street in Helsinki; Stassya's presence among us was clearly missed. As we passed a beautiful department store window with crystal and china displayed, as if inviting us in, we all stood and gawked. I could not help but think about our recent experiences, and took in the magnificence as if for the first time. I couldn't resist and went inside as I had spied a set of delicate pink wine glasses with a white rose etched around the side. To my delighted surprise, they were made in Russia! I bought the set, watched as they were carefully wrapped, and hand-carried them the rest of the way home.

The next day, our flight home was uneventful. Upon landing and arriving in the terminal at Los Angeles, several of the boys leaned down and kissed the ground. We all stood before the "Welcome to America" banner and had Jim take our picture. Tom and Lilka, from CHI, surprised us by flying from San Francisco to Los Angeles in order to accompany us on our connecting flight home. Even though exhausted from our long flight, we all talked at once, telling them of our experiences, since there had been no way to correspond with our families at home. Long-distance telephone calls overseas were much too expensive and unreliable, and uncommon at that time.

We were met in San Francisco by the parents of the students, and spouses or friends of the adults. Hugs and kisses, laughter, and tears abounded. Excitement radiated from the gate where we were met and all were relieved that we were home safe, well, and in good spirits. Every single piece of our luggage had arrived, too!

PART TWO: The Wait

15. Sasha

"Dr. Israel, I'm so glad to know that Joshua had a wonderful time," I said in my telephone call to Joshua's father a few days after we had landed in San Francisco. "I enjoyed having him. He contributed so much to our experience with his knowledge of history, his great sense of humor, and his ability to interact with everyone in the group. However," I continued, "this call is of a different nature. I am going to ask you a question and would like you to think carefully about it, and, of course, to consult the rest of the family."

"Go ahead, Mrs. Peebles," he said. "I think I know what you are going to ask, and if I am correct, the answer is yes, we will accept Sasha to come and live with us, as long as he needs us. We discussed this already after Joshua came home and told us about the request from Sasha's mother at dinner. Our family made a unanimous decision that, if asked, we would be happy to bring Sasha permanently into our family. In fact, I took it upon myself to consult with the principal of Marin Academy High School about a full scholarship for Sasha. It was met with great enthusiasm by the staff," he continued. "Go ahead and do what you can to expedite Sasha's visa. We will take care of the rest."

I was humbled at the generosity and love of this family and got to work. It was not difficult to obtain a student visa for Sasha, and soon he was on his way to America and a new life. But first we received a nice letter from Sasha's father translated by Sasha.

~   ~   ~

[From Mr. Berson in Leningrad:]

May 17, 1991
Dear Gayle and Jim!
That was very pleasant to get a letter from you through Tom

Areton. It was delivered much more quicker than by post.

We are glad that you are fine and that you have such interesting and different plans for your nearest vacation. Your life is really changing rapidly. We are glad that you expect twin grandchildren. Good luck!

We wish Sasha to be able to start his own life from the best starting point. And his and our dream is very close to the reality. We were really impressed by your warm words about friends that would be with Sasha in good times and in need. One more time thank you for everything you have done and excuse us for troubles you have got.

We are very sorry that non[e] of us have met Tom Areton while he was in Leningrad. We just knew nothing about this visit. Please, tell him "Thank you!" from us.

Several words about our life. Sasha keep busy preparing for different exams, getting air flight ticket etc. Jenia will go with his kindergarden group to the "summer datcha." In the beginning of summer we are going to start constructing of a small country house, 60 km from Leningrad. So work there, probably will occupy all the spare time.

We hope that soon Sasha would be able to relay our regards to you in person.

Sincerely, Vladimir Berson

P.S. All the flight information Sasha wrote at his letter to the Israel family. He sends his best regards and translated this letter. Luba and Ida send best regards too.

~   ~   ~

Several months after Sasha arrived in 1991, Jim and I sponsored his father Vladimir who worked diligently at learning English while at menial jobs in San Francisco. This man, who had published texts on engineering in Russia, did what he had to, to survive. He washed dishes in restaurants and cleaned offices at night, among other things. When he had mastered some broken English, he came to visit us in our home. During one special family dinner Jim and I had for him, Vladimir sat up straight and proudly announced,

"I going to sponsor my wife Luba, my son Jenia, and my mother-in-law Ida. I have good job, at last, and we have been away for too long."

Jim stood up and, holding his glass high said, "Vladimir, I am humbled by your extraordinary effort to make a better life for your family. You have gone from an intellectual life in Russia to a poor

67

working man's life in America. You have succeeded in learning a new language, and to advance yourself to a place where you can support your family in a new country. I am proud to have been part of this success story." Jim bowed to Vladimir as we all clapped and chimed in together with *Nazdorovie* ["Cheers"].

Back then, Vladimir did go on to sponsor the rest of his family and, within five years or so, they made a new home for themselves in South San Francisco while immersing themselves in learning English.

Our reunion dinner at Fisherman's Wharf, San Francisco.
Back row: Sasha, Vladimir (father), Tom Areton, Stassya, Jim
Middle row: Luba (mother), Lilka Areton, Helen, me.
Front row: Ida (grandmother), Jenia (younger brother).

16. Letters from Leningrad 2

[From England]:

October 24, 1990
My dearest Gaylochcka!
I am in England. I think maybe letters from this part of the world will be lucky in crossing the Atlantic Ocean. I think I was wrong to put in one letter a small peace of a birch tree's cover. It was so white and black. I couldn't stand the temptation. My second letter carried some dried leaves from the park you like so much. Maybe they were stopped by customs or maybe this is something wrong in general with all our services. In the fall we couldn't send parcels anyplace in the S.U. [Soviet Union]. *Thousand of boxes and parcels were standing in piles. Letters were unsorted and I didn't get even my wedding greeting cards* [anniversary] *which were sent by my friends in Leningrad. People who worked at the post offices were nonofficially on strike. They got very small salary and stopped working. Thousands of letters arrived and nobody delivered the mail. I think they would not be able to recover. Sometimes when I look around I wonder why something is still working. I start feeling crises. But we have got what we have built. Our modern society is just the reflection of our primitive ideology. (Have you read* The God's Heart *by Bulgackev?) I am writing so openly now because I am not at home. I think the army is still too strong and they won't coop with loosing their populararty. We can have what it was in Chily* [Chile] *under Penotchet* [Pinochet]. *I am not very much afraid, but some things puzzled me. We have elected people to do things in our city councel, but they are wasting their time discussing problems like should be the name of Leningrad changed, what kind of flag old or new one we should have and so on. They pass laws which don't*

69

work. Everybody has become money-minded and they sell Russia peace by peace. We are a country of funny thieves. This year we had big misfortune - good harvest. Much time was spent on talking how to save (not to harvest) the crop and half of it was lost. Our republics were so happy to get independence that now they are as proud as feudal kings. The local presidents passed the laws forbidding the farmers to sell goods and food to Russia. Tons were spoiled deliberately and rotten.

In September it was a problem to buy potato cabbige, eggs, meat, cheese, bread, sugar. Our supermarket was emptier than you saw. My new one is still not opened because they don't have enough things to pretend that they have plenty. It took me more time dayly to supply my family with something. Prices are so high that we don't panic at all. They are above our understanding. I think that when I return we'll have more problems. I hope the winter will not be too cold. In such situation family has become more important I want to spent as much time at home as it possible. But this year I have 28 hours weekly and Helen is very busy at school. We began playing piano. Twice a week she has piano lessons, and once a week painting, drama circle and dancing. So, I stay with her at school till 5 p.m. Every day I am at school from 8 a.m. till 5 p.m. This is in short about my life at home. But as you understand I am in England now. I enjoy every minute of my stay here but I was happier with you... [Stassya indicated that her hosts didn't seem that interested in her stories, but Stassya enjoyed reading their collection of books from their travels and loved the rural setting of their home. There was a group from this hosting school expected to come for a visit, but Stassya was sure this family would not take part in it...] *But be aware that when I go to bed I say "Good morning Gayle" and when I wake up "Good night, darling."*

Kiss dear Jim for me. Your friend, Stassya

~   ~   ~

My mind was reeling—*they have virtually no food!* Little Helen was already so pale and thin that you could almost see through her. Besides Stassya's hours of work, upkeep of her home and family, spending time with her mother, and preparing lessons, how could she set aside time to stand in line for what little food she could find? With winter coming on, I grew more and more concerned. I wondered, *could we invite Stassya and Helen to come and visit? The process would take too long for this winter, but maybe next year?*

~   ~   ~

70

[From Leningrad]:

November 26, 1990
My Dearest Gayle!
I wish I had more time to write letters to you as often as I want to. It has become a good tradition with me to talk to you dayly, sometimes it seems to me that you are the only person who cares and understands. But we were always pressed for time in California and in Leningrad. I hope you have got my two letters from England. It is really worth seeing: traditions, history, culture all mixed together. I tried to get every new idea, view and I enjoyed my trip greatly. My English hostess corrected all my mistakes, we had exercises in usage and abusage. Her husband helped her with all his might and maybe so you must charge if they have succeded or not. I hope that my charms are not in my mistakes. When I returned I forgot about the English fairy tale at once. I have come just in time to be at the funeral. Paul's father has died. It took much time, strength to do everything in a proper way. Then school began. This year I have 32 lessons every week. It is very tiring but it is necessary if I want to stand prices of the market, which are 10 times higher. Cares and worries about the house take all my time plus Helen with all her activities. Sometimes I feel myself like a Jack from the proverb: "All work and no fun [play] *makes Jack a dull boy."* [James Howell's *Proverbs on English, French and Italian, 1659*]

I don't like dark and gloomy winter with the slush and frost every other day. I miss blue sky and sunshine and warmth and green. That's why I try to keep as much flowers on the window as it possible. Some of them are going to blossom. It can't be compared with your wonderful balcony. (I often enjoy the picture of you two among the flowers) but still something....I heard on T.V. that Mr. [George H.W.] *Bush asked Americans not to come to the S.U. because of the crises and all that. What do you think about it? Can it stop our exchange in August?* [The second homestay in Russia planned for summer 1991.]

With great love Stassya
My best wishes to Jim and your family.

~   ~   ~

My idea had started to take form. I didn't want Stassya to think we were taking pity on her and her situation; however, I wanted to feed her and Helen and give Helen lots of vitamin C. Jim and I had discussed the possibility of having the two of them come for the next

71

winter. I told him that I could use Stassya in my new position with CHI. I was just beginning to develop the Outbound Program of sending American High School students to study abroad. I had been told that I could work out of my home, and I needed an assistant who could help me put the materials together to prepare the students for their year abroad. Who better than Stassya with her wide knowledge and interest in the history and cultures of other people! Therefore, after receiving Stassya's last letter and much research and planning, we offered to sponsor Stassya and Helen for a six-month visa, and I also offered Stassya a small salary to give her some pocket money. We suggested that they come sometime in October or November of the following year and stay until spring.

Shortly after we had started with these arrangements, our letters stopped crossing the sea. That is when I saw my matching dress on television one Sunday morning in early May! I never watch television on Sunday mornings, but for some reason, while waiting for Jim to get ready to leave the house, I turned it on and found myself flipping through the channels.

Then, suddenly I stopped channel surfing. Though the introductory comments sounded dull, it was live from St. Petersburg (as Leningrad had been renamed), and got my attention.

"This is a live simulcast between a panel of professional people in St. Petersburg and one in San Francisco," a commentator said. "The subject is water quality in the bays of both cities."

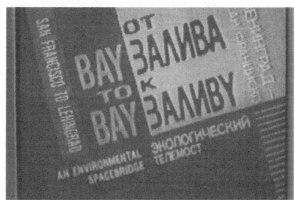

Bay to Bay simulcast, a Sunday morning, May 1991

I was interested enough to continue watching for a few minutes. I couldn't believe my eyes! As the camera panned the Russian audience, there was my matching dress, on the screen! Or was I imagining it?

72

"Honey, I think I saw Stassya in our dress on the TV! Come quick!" I shouted out to Jim.

"What dress?" Jim questioned as he peeked out of the closet.

"Our dress, mine and Stassya's, hurry!"

"No way, on TV?" he shot back. He ran over and stood in front of the television screen. Once again, the camera was scanning the small audience in St. Petersburg, and sure enough, there was my dress!

Jim grabbed a tape, slid it into the tape player and began to record the show. With our noses glued to the screen, we watched carefully for another glimpse of my dress. It wasn't long before we knew it was Stassya, with some of the Russian students from her class who had been with us in 1989! As Jim and I stood there holding on to each other, we hungrily watched the screen for another look at our beloved friend.

"I can't believe it! I simply can't believe it!" We both shouted and pointed at the screen as the camera once again swept over the audience, bringing two of the female students in for a close-up before switching to the San Francisco audience.

"Why are Stassya and the students there?" Jim puzzled.

"I think they are trying to tell us something," I said, "or why would Stassya be wearing one of our matching dresses? I haven't heard from her in such a long time, I'm worried."

"I think she is trying to tell us she is okay," Jim said, clutching my hand. "But how would she even begin to think we would see this program and that she would be on camera?" That question was answered much later.

When the forum ended, we watched the tape over and over again. At the point where Stassya was shown wearing her matching dress, Jim stopped the frame and took a photograph of her so we could study it with a magnifying glass. I printed it immediately and held the photograph over my heart as if I could convey to her that I had seen her and was hugging her close. (Our television remains off Sunday mornings as it always had been before that strange and curious day.)

Soon after that surprising experience, the letters started going back and forth again, and judging from the date on her next letter, Stassya must have written it right after she appeared on television.

~   ~   ~

[Sent from Sweden:]

May 30, 1991
My dearest Gayle!
I have two minutes to write and chance to send this letter with group from Sweden. In May I looked at the dates and according to your plan in thoughts visited all places of interest in Great Britain. I am sure you like it very much. Did you manage to see Sue and get my present? The idea that on your return home another letter and some small gifts were waiting for you (because I had sent them with Tom) pleases me very much.

I am thinking of your kindness all the time. I began to do the nessesary papers for my trip but I didn't think yet where to take that pile of money. Maybe to storm a bank? For a teacher all these amounts of money are too big. I must save for 3 years all my salary. According to the new rate all my month salary can be changed in 15 dollars. Now in the shop I must multiply 30. Humiliating. We were poor now we are beggars. Working from morning till night I even can't feed my child properly. I don't know what to do. But I hope people is free and thanks God without coupons.

My dearest friends. Let us speak about something good! It is very good that we have met. It is great that The Peebles were my host family. This is my fate and I hope that fate is wise. I love you and miss you. Helen sends you her love and thanks for everything. You are so thoughtful. We have so nice presents for every birthday! We have a very nice proverb in Russian. It means that person who gives always gains.

Thank you very much.
Yours Stassya

~   ~   ~

I had sent Stassya cash with a friend who was visiting St. Petersburg to help her with expenses for her trip to us. I had not thought about the difficulty she might have to change those dollars into rubles. Maybe she had to use the black market "mafia" she hated so much.

~   ~   ~

[Hand delivered by a CHI colleague returned from Leningrad]:

June, 1991
My dearest friend!
You are very very thoughtful! I managed to get (using personal

74

ties) a box of Russian chocolates and didn't know how to send it to you. Just of a sudden a person rings me up and informs me that I have a chance to see Barbara from USA with package from Gayle! So, I hope that this wonderful lady will carry a small package to you. He (Volodja – Barbara's host) phoned me in the evening 10:20 and we decided to meet next morning at a certain place. So I am in a hurry to write a "long" letter.

By this time you have met Sue and have spoken to Tom, have got my two letters and can imagine what is situation in Russia. I think it is not very bad but it is because I live here and have patience as all Russian people.

I don't believe that those dealers who have become very rich are thinking about the future of my country. We are country without laws which regulate everyday life, guarantee normal life. The war of laws is very profitable for such people. They manage to gain from everything. We have a very fashionable void now days: barter. Those people who got wealth and power and rights (all 3 go together) try to get something as quickly as possible. They think of today's interest or their own. Our deputies are meeting every day, non-stop meeting. They discuss things pass the laws and the people are sick and tired of discussions. They want actions. People in my country are thinking how to feed a family. According to the pole 60% of population live behind the poverty line. It is very painful that I can't do anything in such situation. Such nice ladies can't speak too much about serious things.

Summer has come and it is very beautiful in Leningrad and in the country. Everything is emerald green. I spend all my weekend in the garden, try to plant, to weed, to dig and so on. Paul has built a very big green house to grow tomatoes. I try to persuade myself that work in the garden is good for my health but my activity parts of my body disagree.

I like when you write about holidays and trips. It is as if I can peep into a fairy tale. I share your social life with you while working in the garden. I wear loose old shapless clothes, rubber boots and so on. Thinking of you at the moment of work I am glad that you can't see me right that moment. I hope that the crops will be good and Helen will eat fruit and vegetables which are good. Now she eats your vitamins. (Thanks Gayle)

Helen has finished her junior school with good marks. Her teachers of music and drawing are pleased with her results. I send you a very funny picture of Helen which was taken in Leningrad *circus during the interval. The little bear is <u>alive</u> and it began to suck Helen's ear. That is why she couldn't but laugh.*

I meet Barbara in the morning. Unfortunately I can't buy anything special. It usually takes much time to find anything. So I send you chocolates, 2 sweets and salt basin.

Helen is in the country with my mother but I looked through her drawings and I like 2 – "Summer" and "Dreamy Horse in the Moon Light". I can't send anything to Jim but my love and special book for notes. I can tell you secretly that I have 2 nice peaces for him, but they are breakable and I can't send them. So I am ready to meet friends from California.

2:30 at night

I have several minutes to write while we are waiting for the train. We went to Petrodvorets (with fountains) together. I had no chance to read your really long long letter about your trip. I read the small part about our friends, your family and our plans. I am doing all the necessary thing with papers but I didn't decide yet whom to rob. I think that I'll find something. I didn't discuss this with Paul. He is very selfish and wants to keep me handy all the time. I'll tell him later when everything is set up.

Send my love to your family and kiss Jim. I am thinking very hard about your suggestions. I want to be with you and help you in every possible way but… Tell me, please, when it is the best time in the fall to come to you (if it is possible). And not to miss the job in CHI. I don't want to be on your account all the time. All the time I am writing to you I am in a hurry or very tired. In general my handwriting is better, but excuse me my darling for it. I hope you manage to understand my thoughts as usual.

Much love, kisses, hugs, Stassya

~　　　~　　　~

At least Helen had some vitamins we sent in our package and the summer garden to hold her over until she would come to us. We were worried that our plans would not work, but we thought just maybe we would be lucky. We hoped.

~　　　~　　　~

76

[From Leningrad]:

End of June, 1991
My dearest Gayle!
When you write letters you describe your trips, your meetings with members of your family, friends, all pleasant events of your life. I am very happy that all your family is so exciting because of the twins who are so wanted. I can imagine how nice and interesting to buy little items for a baby but when you are going to have two babies it must be more interesting. A friend of me has twins a boy and a girl and I remember that when they were born she found it very difficult to take care of them and as much washing was every day she had to hire a woman to help her till they were 2 years.

Is Diane going to do everything herself or you are planning to have a helping hand. When we expect babies we never buy things in advance. Our doctors and medicine system cant give you 100% that everything will be perfect. Many children get serious after effects after their birth and now with all our difficulties people in Leningrad've stopped having babies. I have heard a report over the radio that the rate of birth in Leningrad is lower than the rate of death. It was only the same during the blocade in 1941-1944.

Life is really very hard and lack of hope makes it werse. Our government has done everything to make our life as difficult as it is. We have food copoons on all the main items: meat, butter, flour, sugar, oil, porridge and eggs but we can't buy anything without queing. Very often we can't even buy things we have copoons on. During the winter the government decided to change money – bills of 50 and 100. They wanted to "fight" mafia in such a way. All the bills had to be changed in 3 days. I could change money (but I had only 2 such bills) at my work but all pensioner had to go to the local post office or bank. It was horrible to watch that very very long line of several hundred people standing in cold weather with their sticks all those tired and old people. Usually in Russia all old people have money for their death. They want to be buried in a proper way and they try to keep money in big bills. They think that money is safer in big bills, so they suffered most of all. Several people died in lines, had heart attac, got ill. They were nerveous because it happened that office ran out of money to change and asked them to come next day. But mafia was perfect. They changed their money in dollars and try to do all their business only in hard currency and of course they won. Now we have new rate: I shall pay 27 roubles, 50 copics for 1

77

dollar and 54 roubles for one pound. So if one year ago my month salary was 40 dollars (you remember 1 to 6 was official rate and 1 to 15 black market price) now they pay me according to the new official rate about 15 dollars in month. Though I got 30% rise in salary, on the second of April all the prices went up. We were promised that the rise will be about 40% but when we came to the shop we were more than surprised. I want to write to you the differences.

	Before	Now (in roubles)		Before	Now
meet	2	7	shoes	65	200
butter	3.60	10.50	sweater	100	500
eggs	.90	2.30	coat	250	1,200
potato	.30	1.80	boots	120	700
veg.oil	1.60	3.10	bag	30	180
fish	.90	3.00			

I gave you the prices of the shops prices at the state. Farm markets are higher and of course black market is flourishing. All our bus, tram fares are 2-3 times bigger. And the ticket to America is not 2,000 but 4,000. I think it is more than 40% rise. The government give each person compensation about 60 roubles but it doesn't cover the cost. Now they begin to speak that we must pay money for our flats so to buy them. This is not the law but they think about it. People are very gloomy. Many factories are on strike but in vain. Many plants were closed because they don't have material to work with. All ties were broken, new ones are not to settle down. Our shops are empty. Problems are very ridiculous. I can't mend the underwear because I don't have white thread. If you loose your button it is difficult, not to choose but to find one. And you have to face problems like this all the time. People are tired of them. We exist rather than live.

According to researches of a national agency who have been watching sales of 1100 basic types of consumer goods, only 20 have been available over the counter nationwide. This is less than 2%. 90% of all types of goods are distributed on the basis of ration cards and coupons. People do not believe in stability of supplies so they buy goods five times more than they normally need. We try to stockpile as many as we can because the forcasts are not good.

Plants are not interested earning roubles only in barter or hard currency. So if you need something we have to go to black market and they dictate the price. I explained you how our mafia works. If you don't have chance to buy what you want you'll pay any price. Our political news are not good. All school exchanges are stopped. Our government reported that the officials had rights to read any letter, to listen to the telephone conversation and enter any place and make a search any moment even without a person. I think we are returning to the years of 1937. I feel as a person in a castle who is locked in the room with ceiling going down all the time. Young people see that it is impossible to earn money in the honest way so they begin to rob and steal. Cases of criminal deeds are more often.

I am very afraid of Helen's fate. She is small now but even optimist like me can't see changes for better. They predict even werse. I would like to come to you but I am afraid that it will be very difficult for you and your family. Do you honestly think that I can earn money not to be on your back. Thank you very much for your kindness, thoughtfulness. It is very good to have true friends.
I love you very much. Thank you…Yours, Stassya

~   ~   ~

It sounded to me like the country was falling apart and we might be too late to get Stassya and Helen out of there even for a short visit over the winter. I was so worried that Stassya would give up trying. If not for Helen, I thought she would just quit. It seemed so hard to just exist each day. Despite the fact that I was excited about the coming birth of my oldest son, Andrew's twins, my first grandchildren, my mind was focused on Stassya and her troubles. I could not even imagine how I would have reacted to such a daily struggle. Stassya was strong and an optimist, but I was still worried that she would collapse in a heap and just give up. Worse was still to come.

~   ~   ~

[Hand delivered by Tom on his return from Leningrad]:

Beginning July, 1991
My dearest friend!
It was very clever of you to ask the directory of CHI to deliver your important letter. Thank you, darling – thank you Tom! This is the quickest letter I got from you. Reading it, it felt myself present at your this week family problems. You must be very proud preparing yourself to become the greatest grand-mother in the world. Dianne is so tiny and I can imagine her being round by September. But

everything is very exciting. Andrew tries his best and it must be very pleasant for a woman when you are cared and looked after. Russian women are neglected in such matters. I am getting more and more disappointed. People can't understand that love and care can change their life to the better. They treat you in a good way only when they need you. I met so many times with such things. Now I am in a bus, going to Elena (the vice principal) and write my letter to you because I have only one chance through Elena reach Tom and give him this letter. Elena is allowed to meet Tom by Principal. So excuse my handwriting, you know our roads are very bad. I feel that people living in such difficult situation must help each other, but our people have become very selfish. It is sad. Even my Paul has changed to the worse. That is why your letters, your kindness, friendship, you desire to help is so precious and great! It gives me strength and hope to know that there are kind and wonderful people in the world. When I got your invitation and read lines about me and Helen I couldn't but cry. I understand that it will be very difficult for you to take care of me and my daughter for a period of time. I am afraid that I can't pay you back for your kindness. Do you think that I can be of any help in your work. Please tell me honestly. I love to come and to give Helen a chance what life can be but I hate the idea of being on your back.

Our government humiliates us all the time, even when we are given chance to visit our friends abroad. We can't buy for them nice presents. We are allowed to carry out things not more expensive than 30 roubles. You knew the prices which were in summer, but now they are higher. We are beggers in our own country and we are beggers abroad. We can't buy things at home for our roubles and can't change money into dollars before trip. One dollar nowdays is about 30 roubles. At the black market it is about 35 roubles. So, foreign tourists feel very happy. They can buy works of art, boxes, pictures, can go to the restaurant. I can't do it working day and night for 20 years. I haven't deserved right to buy clothes for my child, to feed her properly. Going along Nevsky Prospect I see more and more signs "hard currency". Everything is for sale. And I can't do anything to save my child from this hostile, money-minded world.

Our meeting has changed my life. I know that nice ideas interesting work, chance to help people are what count in life for you and it is great. Thinking about you I feel better. I pray God for you and your family. Kiss and hug them for me. Yours Stassya

~   ~   ~

I knew Stassya was writing this on the bus and that the roads were bad, but her bungled handwriting at the end of her letter nearly broke my heart. Tears rained down my cheeks (and as I am writing this now, nearly 25 years later, tears are in my eyes). What grief and hopelessness came across in her letter to me from this woman of art and culture, of humor and sense of fun, of love and devotion. I had to take her away from it all, if only for a short while. I could think of nothing else.

~   ~   ~

[From England]:

End of July, 1991
Congratulations!
I hope it is not very difficult to mail these two letters to Great Britain. It takes so long from Leningrad. You know it. (Imagine, on the 13th July I got a letter sent from England written on the 16th of April.)
Dear Grandfather Jim! And Grandmother Gayle!
This is one of the most important event in your life, long waiting event. I am sure that you feel very happy and satisfied. You have a big and nice family and your blood and name will not die. Everything is perfect and looking at your smiling, young, beautiful faces I realize that true love can resist time. Very often I tell my friends about you. All in all I saw you for 6 weeks and I felt as if it had been your honeymoon. I think in your free time (Do you have a hope to find it) you must open a school. "How to love and to be loved after 30 years of marriage". Remembering you and thinking about you I begin to believe that love exist not only in Harlequin books.
Thank you very much for such experience. I am sure that you would be great and perfect grandparents! Your pupil, Stassya

~   ~   ~

I hoped after a possible six months of living with us in close quarters, my dear friend would still feel the same! The pressure was now on for us to be on our best behavior. We had only two bedrooms and two bathrooms. Our television was in our master bedroom upstairs, our washing machine and dryer in the downstairs entryway, my office and workspace was in a small landing area upstairs and often overflowed into our bedroom. There would be very little privacy unlike when we had lived in a large, four-bedroom, three-bath home where we had hosted over thirty people

81

from other countries over a period of twelve years. They had ranged in age from twelve years old to middle-aged businessmen. Some of them were from Japan, Sweden, and Indonesia. They had stayed with us anywhere from about a week to a month at a time. But some had stayed much longer, including a college student from Indonesia, who had rented a room in our home for two solid years while he studied at the local university. Now we were in a small home and were inviting a mother and daughter who would have to share the small, downstairs bedroom in our home for up to six months.

Jim and I looked the downstairs bedroom over. Little did we know the obstacles we would have to overcome as we began to prepare our home for our precious guests. It already had two single beds with a nightstand in between with a reading lamp on it. The bedspreads were a light aqua satin over thick, soft comforters covered in snow-white duvets which we had brought home from Japan. One wall was papered with a Chinese design depicting light green bamboo branches and pale pink cherry blossoms.

Our guest bedroom, ready and waiting....

Across the room was a small glass-topped table with two chairs and a hanging lamp. Next to that we put a tall, narrow rattan bookshelf which we had found in a used furniture store. Then, we had cleared out the closet and fixed one half with shelves and the other half with double rods. The room had a large window and a sliding glass door. Both were covered by aqua vertical blinds, and the door led out to a small private deck. On that deck, we placed a sturdy redwood deck chair with deep green cushions and a little redwood table next to the chair. A small fountain with a ceramic frog spewing water and surrounded with green ferns was the perfect added touch to make it a nice place for Stassya and Helen to relax and enjoy our fall weather.

Come what may, we were ready, in spite of not knowing how or when this would take place.

~   ~   ~

[Hand carried by a friend and mailed from England:]

July 31, 1991
My dearest Gayle!
I have only 2 minutes to write, because I met a person from England who promised to mail my note (I can't name this [in] a letter).
I want to inform my darling that I **have!** *all visas and papers to come to you. (though I had one very shaky moment)* [which Stassya explained to me later]. *The only problem is the tickets but it is matter of time. I'll try to do my best to come in October. CHI group [is] in Moscow. I don't know anything about them yet. Elena (the vice principal) is in Moscow with them. I'll meet the group as soon as they come to Leningrad. I am going to invite Teresa to my house and maybe she'll stay with me for one week-end. I'll send a long letter with her and something.*
I read your last letter (with pictures of "my bedroom"). Thank you for keeping me in touch with all events of your family. I feel that I am among you. I got Joelle's very moving letter. Thank you for your kindness and thoughtfulness.
I kiss you and hug you! Thanks God I remember your address by heart.
Love you, Miss you, Kiss you. Stassya Are we going to meet in October? I cross my fingers.

~   ~   ~

We started to believe that Stassya and Helen might actually come. I was sure that Stassya would be able to find tickets even if she had to do business with the "mafia". Excitement was building on both sides of the Atlantic. I could imagine tsunamis flowing back and forth with the high energy that emanated from the two of us.

But there was still much to do. Somehow, I had to get them from New York to San Francisco. Stassya could not purchase tickets on Aeroflot Airlines for that leg of the journey. I had connections through CHI and thought perhaps I could find someone who lived in New York to help me. Along with Stassya, I crossed my fingers, too.

~ ~ ~

[Hand delivered by the CHI leader of the 2nd group to Leningrad:]

August 15, 1991

> *My dearest Director of Outbound*
> *(it sounds wonderful!)*
> *My happy Grandmother!*
> *(it sounds sweet)*
> *My proud Mother of Prisewinner!*
> *(it sounds great)*
> *My true friend!*
> *(it sounds right)*

This year, my dear, is full of nice and wonderful events in your life. I am very happy for you and thank you very much that you give me chance to share your happiness, worries, success. I know about your visits, meetings and travels and nice pictures help me to imagine everything so clearly as if I were among you. Thank you for me being included.

Yesterday I met Barbara and she gave me your package and money. And I began to cry. I couldn't stop my tears rolling down my cheeks. It was such a mixture of feelings.

*August 18, 1991 (**before** the broadcasting)* [of Gorbachav's fall from power]

Today American group is leaving. I think it is a success. People have become friends and love and understand each other and you are part of it. You must be proud of yourself, my dear peace maker. I can't miss the chance to write to you again because you'll get it so soon.

My life was so calm and smooth. No events, no up or downs. Today is like yesterday and tomorrow is like today. Nothing. You have come like a storm changing everything! It is great. Thank you, my dear friend for all your attempts, worries, help, words, deeds, love, care!

I am looking forward to kiss and hug you. My best wishes to Jim and all my friends.   Lovingly, Stassya

My thoughts whirled around in my head when I read this letter. My letters must read like a novel. I had hoped they did not sound like bragging because that is not what I had intended as I described our trip to Europe and the birth of our twin grandchildren. My *prizewinner* was my daughter, Joelle, who had won a college scholarship. These events must have sounded like a dream to Stassya and I wanted to share my life with my new friend. I could have pushed her away; instead, she kept waving my flag and sending loud hurrah's across the ocean. Then all hell broke loose when I opened the next letter in the packet....

~   ~   ~

August 19 (after) [Yeltsin took over the government]

Thank you very much for everything you have done and tried to do. I love you. If anything goes wrong try to help Helen.

My dear Gayle!
I had to open this envelope because it was said over the radio horrible things Gorbachev is not president for the USSR. They set 6 months of....
Dear I can't write English....please ask Jane to read.

So I asked my only Russian-speaking friend Jane about whom Stassya knew, to read and translate Stassya's heart-rending letter:

"For 6 months they announce the state of emergency all over the country, which is the beginning of the military dictatorship. They demand to fight everyone who is trying to weaken and destroy the country. It is the call to start the civil war against anyone who does not share the ideas of the new government. They begin to control everything and forbid the freedom of speech, meetings, press. I think this is the return to the purges of 1937."

Dear, contact Teresa, she knows all the details. I love you. I pray for you. I am afraid that our plan is ruined but even if you don't get letters must know that I love you.
Stassya

85

I was devastated...it was too horrible to imagine. I sat day after day for a week in front of the television in my son's home, rocking two very new, very small grandbabies in my arms, tears streaming down my face. The news was so bad. I had made fun of Gorbachev, even called him Gorby; now I wished him back with all my heart. In my eyes, he was such a hope for Russia, but now I could see that at least many of the Russians thought either he was going too slowly with the changes he was proposing, or did not want changes at all. (I can still see the image of Boris Yeltsin standing on top of a tank in Moscow, with his fist raised in the air.)

I was terrified for Stassya. This could go either way and if it went backwards, I could only imagine that she could be a target for the KGB, since she had been here and also in England. She was a teacher of English, and she had just received her visa to go back to America for a visit. Even if they let her go, would they hold Helen as a ransom to get Stassya to return? Because at this point, with what was happening, I could not see her going back to Russia, at least not for a while, once she arrived in the United States, if she ever did return.

First there had been hope, now it was dashed. It felt as if I were on a ship in distress, rocking back and forth, going down into a deep trench, and cresting the wave at the next moment. This went on for a month. I couldn't even imagine Stassya's fright at the abyss staring her in the face.

The next letter was full of hope, but left me exhausted with doubt. *Please, please come as soon as possible!* I thought.

~   ~   ~

[From Leningrad:]

September 13, 1991
My dearest Gaylorka!
Thank you very much for your wonderful call the day before. I wish I had not been that sleepy. I didn't tell you all what I wanted and now I want to enjoy this chance to send these lines which'll meet your eyes in several days, not weeks or months.

Thanks to the tape with your voice I remember your tones and intonations and they help me to fix up my mind into everything-will-

be-all-right mood.

Now a very charming melody "any time" dominates everything. So it is matter of time and I hope that I'll manage to come before all my visas are over. Helen is looking forward to her trip and this helps me to make her study better. Poor girl read and learned English every day during her summer holidays. The only person who is not happy is Paul but I think he is too selfish. It is very convenient to have everything ready at home and wife handy at home all the time. Shopping is not fun in USSR (but nowdays maybe it will be better to write Russia. Because USSR is not exist any more. And I don't know if it is good or bad.)

Our life nowdays is so misery and hard that it is very difficult to imagine that it could be worse. But they say that we are expecting hyper inflation. But on the 19th of August I realized very strongly that for me it was more important to have chance to correspond with my friends, not to be cutoff by iron curtains or laws from people I care about. Thanks God everything is over and we have hope that our leaders know what to do and what way to choose. But it is very difficult to build democratic society the first hundred years.

I want to come to you as quick as possible not because I am afraid of hardships and misery. I am accustomed to overcome difficulties all my life. I am afraid that in several months tickets will be more expensive than I can pay now. When we came to America 18 months before, the tickets price was 2000 now it is 6000 and I am sure it is not limit.

And I want to help you with your work in the fall when you have a lot of work (or you have plenty of it all the year round). Now your words "anytime" have helped me to feel more relaxed. It is so nice to understand that you are wanted and needed. Thank you for this wonderful chance and hope.

I didn't speak about my trip at school with Nicholas [school principal]. I'll do it when I know the date. At school I have 26 hours every week and very happy that it is not as many as usual. I have only 11th and 8th forms so it is very interesting to work with them. Some of my pupils are really very good and want to study English at the Institute. I like my work and it gives me pleasure to realize that I can teach and develop young heads.

I like to go to our shops trying to find something interesting for you and when I manage to buy nice things it makes me happy.

Thank you for sending two letters to England. It is quicker from California than from Russia. My dear friend I hope that all members of your family young and grown-up are all right. I hug and kiss them all and wish the best of everything. I do hope to see all of you soon.

With love and gratitude, yours, Stassya

~ ~ ~

I was happy to have found someone in New York who was an Area Administrator for CHI. He lived near Kennedy Airport. When I asked him if he would be willing to meet Stassya's flight from Leningrad and give her the two tickets for San Francisco which I would send to him, he said,

"Of course, it would be a pleasure. Send me the tickets and her flight information. I will find her and her daughter and help them on their way to you." So now we just had to wait for Stassya to receive her two precious tickets from Leningrad to New York.

~ ~ ~

[Hand-carried from Leningrad by Barbara of CHI:]

End of September, 1991 [Stassya's last letter before her arrival]

My dearest Gaylochka!

It is very difficult to believe but everything seems that I can come! You are miracle! Not typical American! You have done it. You always manage to do what you want (can it be dangerous?)

I met Barbara for several minutes in the car and when we were alone she handed me an envelope with money from you...I can't describe my feelings or a mixture of feelings but I couldn't stop my tears. You have been taking such a great care of me. I am not accustomed to. You are spoiling me and my daughter spending your time and money on us. I hope that members of your family are not jealous. I know you'll understand all my worries because you surprisingly understand me better than others. I am dreaming about our long long hours speaking and speaking and speaking. It is a real happiness when you can be understood. Now I need you, your calmness, you advise. And I want very much to be of help for you.

All my papers are done. Passport and visas are got. I am allowed to enter USA till 12.01.92. [January 12, 1992] *I am on the waiting list for the tickets since July. They say it takes usually 4 months to get tickets sometimes longer but I hope to use personal ties (I hope others don't have them) and come in October. Elena*

88

[vice-principal] *promised to help and as soon as I knew my flight I should inform you using faxs or telephone. And I hope to get the information from you what way to start walking towards California. I am writing and can't yet realize that I am speaking about my plans. I cross my fingers and pray.*

I don't know what to do with my work. It depends on the day of my leave and the date of my returning. But holiday can't be that long. Shall I relieve or maybe Nickolas [the principal] *will fire me with great joy? I am not afraid of being jobless after my returning but everything is not clear Paul included. I began to hint him about the possibility of going to America with Helen but he is not very happy to discuss it. I feel myself like a spy acting secretly according to the plan.* [At this point, Paul still didn't know of Stassya's plan to come to the U.S.] *My mother will miss Helen and me. Helen is afraid of new school foreign children and the language. So everybody worries. But I want so badly to change something in my life just for some time. You give me hope and I know that this is the most precious gift in life. Thank you very much. I am thinking constantly what can I do for you in return.*

I tried to explain what kind of mixture of feelings was in my heart when Barbara gave me the envelope. A big yellow package followed. And when I opened it at home it was funny to think how many nice beautiful useful things would be kept for years without being opened. They are so nettly packed! By the way I still keep soap, matches, perfums and all what was packed. I opened your box of sweets only when I got visas from USA to celebrate the event. With mother and Helen we cut every sweet. Helen keeps the box. She puts her small treasure in it. I think I must start opening beautiful boxes and tear nice wrapping paper. (I remember how your boys began to tease me during Christmas spoiling piles of beautiful paper). Among all my treasure I keep all your letters so nicely printed. They are of all colors and preserve so much information about your life, travels, impressions and very often I reread them. It makes me so happy. It is so nice to realize that under the same sky and the sun there is a person who shares everything with me and I want to do it in return hundred-fold.

I think this year is a very happy one for your family. So many nice and important events. Let it be so in future. My life is not very colourful. I can hardly remember anything very important or nice. This summer I spent at my small wooden crooked house, trying to supply family with frest berries and vegetables. I am not good at

89

farming or maybe don't like it very much so it took too much time and energy. I can't say that my harvest will last long in October. Everything will be eaten but at last I didn't buy anything in summer. Helen is happy in the country. There is a small river to bathe in, a nice forest to go to, bycicle to travel about and no school so paradise. I couldn't but spoil her holidays a little teaching her English. We managed to study 9 tenses in the active voice and 3 tenses in the passive voice. Present Perfect is the most troublesome fellow in your grammer.

This spring was very wet and cool and this is why green trees and bushes were very fresh the whole summer. The grass was very thick and long and I didn't want to weed such beauty but I had to. July was very warm and sunny. Helen and me went everyday swimming and I got a good tan. August brought many rains and rainbows, beautiful dark sky with bright stars at night. Sometimes it is so amusingly cloudy. Clouds are of all colours – from white till dark grey and they are so shaped. We find funny animals and castles and what not with Helen. Helen writes a book about foxes. It has already 26 chapters and many pictures.

My dear Gayle, thank you very much for your coming into my life. I hope to see you soon. Best wishes for all members of your family. My special hug to Jim.

With love, yours Stassya

~   ~   ~

"I am coming, I am coming! I have tickets, I am coming!" These were the first words I heard over the telephone which crackled and buzzed in my ear—words like sweet honey. I took down the flight information, told Stassya about our contact in New York at the gate, that someone was going to help her get on the connecting flight to San Francisco, and then we were promptly cut off. But at last she was coming and in less than one week! I would have to scramble to buy those tickets and send them via overnight mail to New York.

My fingers were still crossed when I got the call from my contact Richard in New York that Stassya's flight was delayed due to heavy fog in Leningrad. So we waited once again. Then at last, early the next morning, Richard called again, this time informing me that the flight was in the air, and he would return to Kennedy airport to meet Stassya with a sign at the gate saying "Gayle" in very large letters. I had never met Richard, but he was an angel who appeared in my life just when I needed him. He made sure Stassya received the tickets and called to tell me that she would be on the morning flight to San Francisco.

The next morning, Jim and I got up early and raced to the airport, two hours away, so we would not be late to meet our precious friend and her daughter.

PART THREE: The New American

17. Welcome to our Home

After we arrived at the airport and parked the car, we checked the arrivals board for the gate number and then went directly to the gate to await our guests. I had on my matching dress as it seemed to have become a tradition that we would wear them on special occasions, and this was **definitely** the most special of occasions.

I spotted Stassya first, ran to her and hugged her close for a long time. She was a gift to me and, of course, was wearing the matching dress, too! Little Helen stood to one side, patiently waiting her turn to be held and loved by us. Jim had waited, too, for *his* turn. We laughed and all talked at once, but I could see the fatigue written all over Stassya's face, and Helen looked as though she would fall asleep at any moment. We grabbed their carry-ons, went downstairs to retrieve the one piece of luggage Stassya had checked, walked out to the car, and drove home.

I had hot soup, warm bread, and some grapes ready in just a few moments. We put Helen to bed, kissed her good-night, and talked for an hour before we sent Stassya off to bed.

The next morning we let them sleep as long as they wanted. Around 11 a.m., mother and daughter emerged from their room looking refreshed. We had a special brunch planned out on our upstairs deck overlooking the oak trees. There were dozens of pots of flowers everywhere. Big black bumble bees were buzzing around the lavender which put out a lovely scent in the air. We sat at our round umbrella-covered table. I had decorated the table top with a ceramic frog and a vase of marigolds. The sun was shining and all was well with our world. Helen looked all around her with wide eyes and a happy smile on her face.

"I must be sitting in one of my picture books," she said in Russian which her mother translated for us.

We laughed and chatted as we ate the cheese and veggie quiche served with crispy bacon and accompanied by perfectly ripe slices of cantaloupe. After we finished with tea and toast, Jim, with his trusty camera, posed us in front of various pots of flowers and took lots of pictures.

And when we leaned back to relax and drink our mimosas, Stassya told us of their horrible experiences at the two airports:

"I have never seen such fog in Leningrad," she began with a big sigh. "It was so thick, you couldn't see nothing. As soon as we arrived at the airport in Leningrad, we heard the flight was delayed. No one told why or how long. Then to keep us away from the foreigners who were also waiting for flights, we were taken to a small room with few seats and told to wait. My dahlings, there was no food, no water, and one small toilet room."

Stassya took a sip of her mimosa, licked her lips in ecstasy, closed her eyes, and continued,

"You know I am a typical Russian mother. I took snacks for Helen and some juice. We sat on the floor with our backs against the wall. After a long time, Helen laid down and put her head in my lap. Lucky girl, she slept while I sat and worried. I had thoughts of all the things that happened to keep me from coming to you. I have not even told you all!"

I looked at this beautiful, brave woman sitting at our table telling us of her ordeal and her determination to bring little Helen for this experience of a lifetime. I filled Helen's glass with more orange juice and offered her another piece of toast and jam. She smiled, enunciated very slowly, and carefully said, "Thank you." I replied with a formal, "You are welcome," and then thought to myself *it won't be long and you will be chattering in English, my little one.*

"You see, my dahlings," Stassya went on, "you sponsored two of us, Vladimir and myself at the same time. As fate would happen, I was standing in a long line outside of the American Consulate to apply for my travel visa to America and was shocked to see Vladimir Berson [Sasha's father] standing in the same line ahead of me, apparently to apply for his visa papers. Unfortunately, our sponsor was the same person, and our letters were signed by the same, now to be famous, Gaylochka."

Stassya looked at me with loving eyes assuring me with her look that she knew I was only trying to help.

"I realize you couldn't know that we both would apply the same day, but I was shaking," she went on, as I listened in horror at what it may have cost both families!

"I was so nervous," she continued, "because I was sure that since Vladimir was there first, he would get his visa and I would be told 'no', or even worse, that we would both be pulled out of line and accused of showing false letters. I could just hear the big thump as the stamp would have hit my letter with large, red letters—DENIED." She said this with a nervous laugh.

Weeks after that frightening experience, both received their visas, but not before the stress of waiting wore them down. I, of course, had been completely oblivious of the possible consequences of the timing involved regarding the two sponsorships, and was now surprised they had both gone through!

Then, the revolution happened....

"Dahlings," Stassya began in a more serious voice, "when something bad happens in Russia, the radio buzzes, and the television goes black. After that, the music of "Swan Lake" plays over and over and over without stopping. The Russian people know that something is wrong. We sit and wait to hear what happened. Sometimes it is the harvest, sometimes someone is assassinated, sometimes a plane crash, but this time I thought it may be political because of what was happening in our country."

Stassya took another sip of her drink, wiped the tears that were beginning to form with her napkin, gulped, and continued, "I was frightened more than I have ever been in my life. That is when I wrote the letter I sent to you in Russian. I was so afraid that I could not concentrate or think in English. I knew the group was leaving that day so I quickly wrote it and managed to get it to Theresa before the group left for the airport."

Helen looked from one of us to the other as Jim and I were as visibly upset as Stassya. I had forgotten that she was listening without understanding a word. Stassya stopped then and leaned over to Helen, kissed her on the top of her head, and spoke to her in Russian. Helen looked relieved. I caught my breath as Stassya said we would continue later.

"We have lots of time to talk, let's get settled and play a little," she added.

Jim took Helen to play in the swimming pool at our clubhouse area while Stassya and I worked at getting the two of them settled into their room and talked about our plans to enroll Helen into the local school in a few days.

That evening after Helen had gone to bed, Stassya continued her story,

"One day Paul, Helen, and I rode our bicycles out in the country near our *dacha* [the wooden house Stassya's father had built]. We were surprised to see that rows and rows of barracks were being built. They were not so fancy and Paul said it looked like a concentration camp." Stassya let out a deep breath and went on, "That is why when I heard "Swan Lake" begin to play on the radio and television, I was sure someone would come for me and put me there. I thought all our plans were ruined. I was scared for Helen. I didn't think Paul or my mother could care for her. I wanted her to have a normal life or at least to see what a normal life could look like even if it was for a short time."

Stassya stood up, pushed herself away from the table and headed to the kitchen.

"Now, let's have a cup of tea. I will tell you some Russian jokes about the situation going on now. Russians love to make jokes about their circumstances since they can do nothing."

I managed to come out of the hypnotic-like state I was in, caught my breath, and joined Stassya in the kitchen.

And so, once again, Stassya managed to lighten the mood, and we went to bed that night laughing and looking forward to the next day and the next and the next.

18. Settling In

We waited a few days so Helen would feel comfortable with us, and then took her to our nearest elementary school to enroll her. She was put into the fifth grade. The following week, we spoke with the school bus driver and explained about Helen's lack of English and asked about the route. He was very kind and told us not to worry. He would be sure she was on his bus, and he would let her off at the stop nearest our home, which was only one short block from the bottom of our hill. I showed Helen where the bus stop would be and walked up the hill with her. She could remember our house easily as it was the first one upon walking up the hill.

Everything had gone smoothly until a few days later, when Stassya and I had a lull in our work and took a break. Stassya decided to go meet Helen's school bus for the first time, so she could walk her home. In the meantime, the school bus had gone up another street and let Helen off at her usual stop closer to our home, and Helen had walked to our home by herself. She knocked on the door.

I let her in and, in a flash, she dropped her backpack, and flew out the front door crying, "Momma! Momma!" over and over again. I ran out after her and caught her in my arms with her back to me. We were near the mailbox where she could see down the hill. I wrapped my arms around her as she moaned, and it occurred to me that she may have thought her mother had tricked her and brought her to America to give her away and then leave to go back to Russia without her!

Helen was very aware of the bad conditions in Russia and she could not understand us when we were talking. Perhaps, she had thought we were making secret plans to have Jim and I adopt her.

Who knew what fearful thoughts had gone through the child's mind! I held her tight, as I feared she could run faster than I, and would disappear amongst the trees and brush on the hillside, if I let go of her.

I knew she could not understand me, but I tried to comfort her in a soft singsong voice. "She is coming. She is coming," I said. "Momma is coming. Wait here. Look, she will come up the hill. She is coming. She is coming." I kept repeating this, as I rocked her.

Helen finally quieted down, but tears continued to spurt out of her eyes and run down her cheeks. I found myself crying as well. I could feel her thin, little body trembling as I held her close to me, and then...I felt her body relax as if she had given up.

"*Nyet, nyet*! She is coming," I said, using the only Russian words I could remember in my desperate need to comfort her. "It is okay," I sobbed.

And then...there was Stassya running up the hill! Helen broke away from my arms and ran fast down the hill, throwing herself into her mother's arms. Stassya assured Helen that she was not going away—never, never. She wiped Helen's tears and mine with her handkerchief. We three went inside.

As it turned out, Stassya had walked around the corner and down the street to the *city* bus stop; she, therefore, missed seeing the school bus and continued to wait at the city stop, thinking the school bus was probably late, not realizing she was at the wrong bus stop.

After this had all been cleared up, Stassya suggested we have a nice cup of tea and the molasses cookies she had baked that morning. Thus began our ritual of a "nice cup of tea" for all occasions.

Soon after this, Stassya learned from Helen that only Spanish was spoken on the playground at her school. So as not to confuse Helen and make it more difficult for her to learn English, we decided to enroll her in another school close by. However, this location did not have a school bus for our area, so Stassya and I began to drive Helen to school every day.

It wasn't long before Helen began to make friends. Her first and closest friend was Debbie. Debbie was a bit taller than Helen; she had bangs, blond hair swept back into a pony tail, and she always seemed to have a sweet, welcoming smile on her face. Debbie asked

Helen to join her Girl Scout troop, and Helen was soon selling Girl Scout cookies and, even later on, attended camp for a week. Debbie and her parents Hal and Nancy befriended both Helen and Stassya and became good and lasting friends.

Helen, cookie saleswoman

Debbie and Helen, summer campers

By now we had begun to settle into a daily routine. Jim would go off to work at his usual 7 a.m., and Stassya and I would drive Helen to school, come back to the house, park the car, and go for a walk around the neighborhood. She would try to teach me some Russian words, but it was frustrating because we wanted to talk to each other. Stassya's English was so good and her stories so interesting that I finally called a halt to the Russian lessons.

We would walk for about thirty minutes and then would sit for a cup of tea until 9 am. My office hours were from nine to five, Monday through Friday. The two of us worked in my cramped quarters on the small landing area above our front-door entry where Jim had made me a large table from a shiny, white door. There was room for my telephone, a large bulky computer, printer/fax machine, and filing cabinet. We had to squeeze by each other to reach the telephone and things on the shelves above, and so work spilled over into my bedroom where I had another large table set up with a small

99

file cabinet next to it.

As part of my job, I was occasionally sent to various areas of the United States to speak to groups of area administrators about CHI's new Outbound programs for American high school students. The two programs I introduced were teacher-led groups for Sister School home-hosted short stays or for individual high school students to homestay and study abroad for six months to a year.

As a result of this and my making contact with receiving organizations in France, Spain, Australia, Germany, and England, our department had started to grow, and my and Stassya's work had begun to spill out onto the dining room table and living room sofa, as we printed and collated the excellent, illustrated, cultural booklets that Stassya was researching, writing, and putting together for each student and country. (Eventually, as we continued to expand, I hired my daughter Joelle, newly graduated from college, and rented office space in a nice, nearby complex.)

One misty morning, as Stassya and I started our walk down the hill, she caught sight of a patch of wild mushrooms growing under one of the oak trees along the way. She immediately dropped to her knees.

"Oh my, look at this! I can make you mushroom soup for dinner tonight!" Stassya said in an excited voice as she reached to pick a beautiful white mushroom.

"Oh dear, don't touch those!" I burst out in a horrified voice. "Our wild mushrooms are not like yours in the Russian forest. The ones that grow around here are like your red mushrooms."

I helped Stassya up and made her promise me that she would never pick wild mushrooms. Then I went on to explain that many people new to our area don't realize that some of our mushrooms can be deadly poisonous and that some people had died eating the mushrooms they had picked locally. Stassya was surprised, and, at my insistence, she promised not to pick our local mushrooms. We did manage to have Russian mushroom soup, but that came much later.

19. Helen's First American Holiday

Fall was coming to California. The days were still warm, but the nights were turning chilly. Even in California, we have some fall colors. In Santa Rosa, there are many pastiche trees that turn a lovely red in the fall. There are also liquid amber and maple trees that turn red and yellow before losing their leaves. So it wasn't long before it was time to go out to a farm and pick out the perfect pumpkin for carving. As Helen had no knowledge of our Halloween traditions, she was excited and eager to get started. Joelle and her husband Mike, Jim and I, and Stassya and Helen poked around in the pumpkin patch until Helen spotted the perfect specimen. Joelle also picked out one for herself, as she was to have the privilege of teaching Helen the rudiments of pumpkin carving.

We came home with our two pumpkins and spread newspapers on the kitchen floor. First Helen was instructed to draw the face that she would like to carve on a piece of blank paper. Joelle did the same. After comparing the images, Helen carefully watched Joelle and began with cutting off the top of the pumpkin and setting it aside. Then as Joelle stuck her hand inside the pumpkin and started to pull out the seeds and scoop out the pulp, Helen with her eyes wide open, peered inside, and watched with great interest.

Helen and Joelle scooping

With a giggle and a little bit of hesitancy, she stuck her hand inside of her pumpkin and proceeded to copy Joelle. Helen's little nose was scrunched up as she dug out the insides and checked Joelle's pumpkin once more to see if she was doing it right.

"Now," Joelle said, as she nudged Helen and pointed to her eyes. "Watch me." She picked up the pencil, drew a face on her pumpkin, took the knife and began to poke it into the skin. Helen solemnly followed suit and soon there were two perfect pumpkins grinning at us. Jim was ready with the camera and recorded Helen's first Halloween pumpkin carving.

Two proud pumpkin carvers

We all clapped and cheered. Helen had the most delighted smile on her face, which I don't think came off until after all the Halloween celebrations were over, including finding the best costume to wear and going off to trick or treat in the neighborhood, and then going to see the elaborately decorated haunted house on Santa Rosa's McDonald Avenue.

Choosing the costume Helen would wear to school for the Halloween parade was great fun, as she loved to dress up and pose for pictures. Iris, one of the local CHI Homestay Program Coordinators, loaned us three costumes that she had made for her own daughter over the years.

First, there was the elephant with the long trunk, big pink flappy ears, and a pink ballerina skirt. Helen then tried on the grey elephant costume and held out the big, pink satin ears while Jim snapped a picture. Next, there was the orange pumpkin costume which fit Helen from the shoulders to her knees and had a dark green scarf to tie around her neck as the stem. Again she posed for Jim's camera.

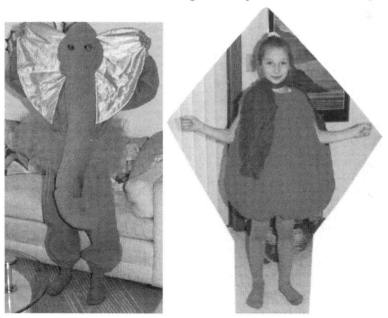

Finally, Helen tried on the black cat costume. She was all in black, from the cap with pointed ears to her feet. Stassya took a black marker and drew cat's eyes on her face, a round black tip on her nose, and outlined her mouth. She added freckles and whiskers that made Helen look as cute as any black kitten could ever be. This was the costume Helen chose.

On the 31st, Helen was dressed extra early to go to school.

103

Stassya and I drove her to school and then we stayed to watch the Halloween parade. I took pictures of Helen waving to us with a big smile on her face.

Trick or Treat!

In the evening, after dark, I put a light in Helen's pumpkin, set it on the deck railing outside the front door and stood Helen there for a picture with her Trick or Treat bag in hand. She was grinning from ear to ear with anticipation. I taught her to say "Trick or Treat" in English which she practiced over and over. We took her out for a walk around the neighborhood and went with her from door to door. Her bag was filled to capacity in no time. Her "trick or treat" had a strong Russian accent to it. I think that, and her sweet kitten smile, was the reason she was getting second and third helpings at each door!

We still had one more activity in mind. One street in our city was popular for the decorations that the neighbors put up every year for Halloween. One house, in particular, on McDonald Avenue, was known as the "haunted house". As we approached the front walkway, we saw a ghost in the window waving and inviting us in. As soon as we entered through the door into the dark house, we could hear the creepy music. A large spider web was waiting for us and seemed to wrap around us just as we spied the huge black, menacing spider overhead. It was illuminated in the light of a candle sitting on a table. We shuttered at the feel of the web as we brushed it, ducked under the spider and continued walking through the house. In one room we noticed a gypsy lady sitting at the table with her hands hovering over her crystal ball; the music was getting louder. When a witch jumped out startling all of us, Helen screeched and hid behind us, pulling her cat's hat right over her ears and covering her eyes at the same time, peeking out through her fingers so as not to miss anything. We taught her a new phrase—"scaredy cat"—which she enjoyed repeating, but only after we exited the spooky house. But then, we were delighted when Helen asked her mother, in Russian, if she could go again!

The evening was finally over, so we headed home, put the tea kettle on, dumped Helen's stash of goodies onto the dining table and checked it all over. Jim and I, and Helen and Stassya each chose our favorites among the many treats and candy bars and sat down to savor our choices with nice hot cups of cinnamon tea.

20. A Day in San Francisco

Jim and I wanted Helen to enjoy her visit with us to the fullest, so one of the first outings we planned was to take the ferry across San Francisco Bay to Pier 1. Joelle went with us. We bundled up and joined the weekend traffic towards the Larkspur Ferry Terminal. We watched as the ferry boat came in and docked.

After the passengers from San Francisco disembarked, we joined the crowd dashing up the ramp and quickly secured a table next to the window. I ordered tea and hot chocolate as we slowly made our way past San Quentin prison and out to the bay. The ferry picked up speed as we passed Angel Island and were approaching the city. It was cold and windy on the outside top deck, but the sun was shining, and we did not want to miss anything. We made our way outside, and all leaned over the railing watching the seagulls flying and dipping close to us as if to say, "Welcome." Joelle and I pointed out Alcatraz, Coit Tower, and the Golden Gate Bridge off in the distance.

Soon, the skyline of the city rose up to greet us as we pulled next to the dock at the Pier 1 ferry building. We walked down the boat ramp, under the clock tower, out across the tram tracks and Embarcadero Plaza, past the Hyatt Regency Hotel to the cable car stop on California Street. We watched and waited as a cable car came down the hill, emptied its passengers, and was positioned by the driver and ticket taker to head back up the hill towards Chinatown and on up to the top to connect to the cable car line that would take us eventually to Fisherman's Wharf. The driver clanged the bell and we dashed to the outside seats along with all the other eager tourists, families with young children, couples holding hands, and local Chinese heading to Chinatown for shopping. When the cable car was full, the driver clanged the bell several times making a melodious tune to signal our departure, and we began the steep climb.

As we approached our connecting stop at the top of the hill, the driver rang the bell several times, grabbed the handle of the brake, and pulled hard to stop, and we tipped backwards making it feel as if we were going to slide back downhill! We then transferred to another cable car and continued in another direction. Helen hung on tight and laughed with delight as we weaved up and down the hills and turned a sharp corner, all on our way to Fisherman's Wharf.

It was lunchtime, so we looked for a place to have clam chowder and San Francisco sourdough bread. After lunch, we walked through Pier 39 and headed to the water's edge to see the noisy seals, a popular spot. The seals entertained us with their antics, nudging and pushing each other for the best spots on the wooden docks they had confiscated from the boat-owners years before. The seals were such pests, climbing up on the boats and making a mess that the owners had given up and taken their boats to another location. Now the seals had the place all to themselves and constantly gossiped and argued with each other with their loud barking, making for great entertainment, as they tried to find the perfect spot on one of the wooden docks to bask in the sun. We watched for a while, and then slowly meandered over to the Ghirardelli Chocolate Factory for dessert.

Since there was a long line, as usual, we had time to study the choices on the menu. Mine was always the Alcatraz Sundae and, since it is large, I always offered to partner up with someone.

"Who is going to be my partner today?" I wondered aloud.

"Not me," quipped Jim. "I am having my usual chocolate with caramel sauce."

"Me, either," seconded Joelle.

Helen had already chosen a strawberry ice cream cone.

"I'll be your partner," Stassya eagerly offered.

We placed our order at the counter, found a table, picked up our napkins and utensils, and, while Jim held our table, wandered over to the large vat of chocolate towards the back of the factory. The chocolate was twirling round and round. It was tempting to stick your finger into the vat to get a lick, but the staff must have realized the temptation and so, unfortunately, it was out of reach. So we made our way back to the counter to watch our ice cream choices being made. The Alcatraz double sundae I had ordered was named and made to look like Alcatraz Island with two large scoops of vanilla ice cream sitting side by side, covered with dark chocolate which hardened as it was poured down across the ice cream. Then we watched as a fog of whipped cream was sprayed all around the rim of the dish and two cherries were placed on top. We brought our dishes back to the table where Stassya licked her lips with anticipation and declared that she was honored to share my sundae.

It wasn't long before she realized that I ate my ice cream very fast so it wouldn't melt, while she wanted to savor each and every bite. When I finished my side of the dish, I began to poke at her half of the hard chocolate since it was so tempting. That was when she learned that it was not the privilege she had thought it would be, to share my ice cream with me!

The Alcatraz

"You tricked me," she said in an accusing voice to Jim and Joelle. They sheepishly smiled, and continued eating their sundaes with one hand wrapped around the rim of their dishes to protect them. Even little Helen who watched in amazement seemed to understand what had happened and laughed with delight at the antics of us "grownups".

We ended our day with a walk through Chinatown looking into the shops and admiring their displays of fans, coolie hats, satin slippers, and Chinese trinkets of all kinds and colors. Stassya and Helen tried on the pointed coolie hats and posed for a picture. We could hear the clanging of the cable cars as they passed Chinatown's Gate and finally climbed aboard one, to head back to the ferry building at Pier 1. We were just in time, as the ferry was waiting at the dock. We dashed up the ramp and found a place at the railing. We watched the pink and orange sunset outlining the city skyline. The Golden Gate Bridge was truly golden in that light, as we stood at the railing, savoring the last few minutes of a magical city and a magical day.

Posing in Chinatown, San Francisco

CHOCOLATE MANUFACTORY AND SODA FOUNTAIN

SPECIALTY SUNDAES

SORRY - NO SUBSTITUTIONS ON SPECIALTY SUNDAES

EMPEROR NORTON . . . Here sits two noble scoops of vanilla ice cream in a throne of hot fudge sauce with bananas towering from all sides . . . robed with whipped cream and crowned with almonds, chocolate chips and a cherry $4.50

GOLDEN GATE BANANA SPLIT . . . Vanilla, strawberry and chocolate ice cream topped with crushed pineapple, sliced strawberries and our very own home-made chocolate syrup. A banana bridge rises above the whipped cream fog with almonds, chocolate chips and cherries $4.50

CABLE CAR . . . A circle of whipped cream with 3 scoops of ice cream: rocky road, chocolate chip and chocolate . . . . . smothered with hot fudge sauce and marshmallow topping. Bedecked with almonds, chocolate pieces and a cherry. All aboard! $4.50

CHOCOLATE DECADENCE . . . So good, it's sinful! Ghirardelli famous hot fudge sauce is layered between 2 scoops of chocolate ice cream . . . . . topped with red raspberry sauce. A ring of whipped cream is loaded with tiny chocolate chips $4.50

ALCATRAZ ROCK . . . Infamous Alcatraz prison emerges from San Francisco Bay. A rocky road and vanilla ice cream island set in a bay of whipped cream armored with a shell of Ghirardelli Chocolate, nut rocks and a cherry $4.50

STRIKE IT RICH . . . Inspired by the famous Gold Rush of 1849, mine your way past vanilla ice cream smothered with our homemade hot fudge sauce. Then spike gold! Dig up almond praline ice cream, butterscotch topping and golden almond nuggets. Topped with whipped cream, chocolate chips, almonds and a cherry $4.50

EARTHQUAKE SUNDAE (Serves Four or More) . . . Enjoy with friends! Split 8 flavors of ice cream and a galaxy of 8 different toppings. Cracks are filled with bananas and whipped cream, scattered with almonds, chocolate bits and cherries $18.95

SUNDAES

CHOOSE YOUR FLAVOR OF ICE CREAM (listed at right)
AND TOPPING: (listed below) LOADED WITH WHIPPED CREAM,
ALMONDS, CHOCOLATE CHIPS AND A CHERRY.

FEATURED TOPPINGS:

World Famous
* Hot Fudge or
* Chocolate Syrup $4.50
* (Made right here in our store)

Marshmallow
Butterscotch
Sliced Strawberries
Red Raspberry
Crushed Pineapple $4.25

ICE CREAM

CHOICE OF CONE OR GOBLET

FEATURED FLAVORS:

Vanilla
Chocolate — Ghirardelli's Own
Strawberry
Cookies N' Cream
Chocolate Chip
Rocky Road
Almond Praline
Mint Chocolate Chip
Coffee $2.95

Single Cone Dipped in Chocolate
and Smothered in Almonds $2.95

MILK SHAKES

Chocolate Shake
Strawberry Shake
Vanilla Shake $3.95

ICE CREAM SODAS

Chocolate Soda with Chocolate Ice Cream
Strawberry Soda with Strawberry Ice Cream
Vanilla Soda with Vanilla Ice Cream $3.50

Root Beer Float with Vanilla Ice Cream $2.50

BEVERAGES

Coffee or Decaf . . . . $.95
Coke, Sprite, Diet Coke, Root Beer . . . . $.95
* Hot Chocolate with Marshmallows or Whipped Cream . . . $1.95
* Hot Mocha $1.95

* Made with Ghirardelli's Ground Chocolate

SINGLE SERVINGS

Single Scoop Ice Cream on a Cone or Goblet $2.00
Single Scoop Sundae $3.75

GHIRARDELLI HISTORY AND LORE ON BACK OF MENU

Menu 1990

21. A Day in Disneyland

Disneyland was next on our list. Jim took a few days off work and, since his mother Florence lived in Southern California, we made arrangements to stay with her. We drove for almost ten hours, entertaining ourselves with singing "My Bonnie Lies over the Ocean" along with Helen. In the car, I also introduced the songs I used to sing with our children when driving: "Hang Your Head Over, Blow the Man Down", "Itsy, Bitsy Spider", "Mary Had a Little Lamb", "One Little, Two Little, Three Little Indians", and many others. When we ran out of songs, I taught Helen the nursery rhymes I could remember: "Little Boy Blue", "Little Tommy Tucker", "This Little Piggy Went to Market", "One, Two Buckle Your Shoe" and so many others.

Along the way, we stopped for dinner near Santa Maria at Anderson's Pea Soup Restaurant. After ordering their house special, Split Pea and Ham Soup, along with corn bread and a salad for each of us, I couldn't help reminiscing. Stassya was amused when I told her that Jim and I had stopped there for soup on the first evening of our honeymoon.

"We could barely afford three days for our honeymoon at that time," I explained. "Soup for dinner was about all we could afford. We even had to borrow Jim's brother Richard's car to drive from Los Angeles to Carmel because Jim's car would never have made it," I continued wistfully.

"Yes, we stopped in Santa Maria for our first night," Jim cut in. "In the morning we could not figure out why it was so bloody cold, until we looked out the window and saw snow covering the parking lot of the motel!"

"And when we got to Carmel," I continued, "it was dark. There was snow on the ground and the whole village was bright with little twinkling lights. They surrounded every door and window of all the shops and little restaurants on the main street for the holidays. I couldn't believe it! I thought I had stepped into a Christmas card." Stassya was translating to Helen almost as fast as I was talking. They both turned up their noses and rolled their eyes, as, by this time in Leningrad they would have been sloshing through lots of deep freezing snow and ice that would last until spring.

I laughed and continued at an even greater pace, waving my arms as I spoke.

"And in the morning, we walked along the beachfront at the end of the main street and it, too, was covered in snow. I think it was the first time it had ever snowed in Carmel, and, I know it has not happened again in 42 years!" I looked over at Jim sitting in the booth next to me as my voice softened.

"To this day, sweetheart," I said, "I think you ordered the snow just for me. Am I right?"

Stassya and Helen were looking back and forth between us, as Jim and I were jumping into each other's discourse. Stassya, of course, understood our conversation, but Helen was watching closely. I realized that it would not be long before she would understand us and join in.

"Yes, dear," Jim said, nodding and patting my hand, "But of course."

By this time, we had finished our delicious soup and paid our bill. Jim left a tip, slid out of his seat, grabbed his jacket, and continued in a jolly voice, "And now it is time to finish our long drive. We still have two hours to go. Come on, you three ladies." We all held hands as we skipped out to the car and climbed back in.

As we began driving into the desert area with rock and scrub on all sides, and mountains and desert mingling on one side, the endless horizon on the other, it was amazing to see the home of Jim's mother Florence appear in the midst of it as if a mirage. It was nearly dark when we arrived in Apple Valley which is in the high desert area east of Los Angeles. As we stepped out of the car in the driveway, we could not help but gasp at the wide expanse of the evening sky with its display of zillions of stars beginning to appear.

The adobe style of Florence's home was painted in the soft pink color of a sunset with a deep green lawn of grass leading up to the welcoming sight of Florence with her dignified companion Lady, a full-sized, pure white poodle, expertly groomed, waiting for us on the front stoop.

"I feel as if I've already met you since I've heard so much about you and have seen all your pictures," Florence said with a smile on her face and in her voice after being introduced to Stassya and Helen.

"Please make yourself at home and come have a cup of tea and a piece of my apple pie," she continued as she stepped aside and motioned for us to come in. Helen bent down to pet Lady, embraced her, and became Lady's chosen companion for the duration of our visit.

The next morning, Florence gave Stassya a tour of her lovely home. The glass-enclosed sunroom at the back of the house, with its white wicker furniture, looked out to a lush green lawn. In the middle of the lawn was a fountain surrounded with red roses in full bloom. Jim's father, Jim senior, had passed away earlier that year. He had had a special feeling for roses. They still seemed to bloom enthusiastically and in great profusion just for him, as though continuing to honor his memory. I dearly missed him on this, my first visit since his funeral.

This was the desert, so beyond the green lawn was a chain link fence surrounding the whole property. The ground on the vacant lots all around outside the fence was dry. Nothing seemed to grow there but cactus, tumbleweeds, and rocks. Brown, prickly tumbleweeds had rolled in and were pressed against the fence, as if to see what was going on, and then they quickly reached out for the constant wind and went on their way. Other homes along the street had palm trees and flowers of every color planted in the front like exclamation points among the native cactus that poked up, proud sentinels guarding the beautiful, well-tended homes. I suspect those cactus were held in high esteem by the local residents, since other things had been planted around them with nothing done to discourage their presence.

We spent the first day chattering and eating Florence's excellent cooking and feasting on her delicious apple pie. Stassya asked Florence lots of questions about her recipes and how to use the different spices, and, most of all, how she made her apple pie. As we had already consumed the pie Florence had made for us, she and Stassya worked together to make another just like it.

Helen was enjoying playing with Lady, tossing the ball and

petting her. Lady would tip her head to the side when Helen spoke to her in Russian as if questioning those new words. Then Lady would nudge Helen to toss the ball again, so she could find it and bring it back to her new playmate. Jim and Helen took Lady out for a long walk before Florence's usual five o'clock announcement of "wine time".

We all sat on the front porch with our glasses of wine. Helen with her glass of apple juice had Lady lying at her feet. We watched the magnificent orange sunset as it softened into pink streaks across a vast sky, uninterrupted by leafy trees or tall buildings. As the stars came out one by one, we reluctantly got up out of our comfy chairs, took our empty glasses, and ambled into the dining room for another sumptuous meal.

We spent the next two days in Disneyland as we could not possibly see it all in one day. Disneyland is touted as the "happiest place on earth". That says it all for me as it brings back wonderful memories that began as I celebrated my fifteenth birthday in Disneyland with my best friend Carol. It was in July during the first week it opened in 1955. We both had on our '50s fashionable Bermuda shorts and knee-length socks. We practiced our sassy technique and flirted with all of the young guys manning the rides. We screeched and jumped back when attacked by crocodiles in the Jungle Ride. We screamed when the roller coaster inside Space Mountain reached the top of the first incline and started down the other side at exhilarating speed. It was dark and we could see nothing! Everything was fun and magical that day. (You still hear jokes about the "E Tickets", but that was not a joke. You paid an entrance fee and then bought the ticket book with A- E tickets with the E tickets being for the "big rides" like the roller coasters.)

Disneyland was also where Jim and I dated a few years later. We would spend the day there riding on our favorite rides, sitting and licking our ice cream cones, and holding hands. In the evening we danced in the outdoor pavilion located in the main square outside the castle. It was lit up with little twinkling lights and had a live band. It was very romantic.

Because it was so special to me, I was delighted to share this fairyland with Helen and Stassya. I loved the look on Helen's face when we walked through the gate and looked down Main Street to the Sleeping Beauty Castle. Her eyes were wide open as she looked around with awe and wonder. I can't even imagine what she thought, as the contrast was so vast from the old European elegance of the

114

Leningrad I had seen. Even for me, it was like stepping into another place in the universe.

After Jim took our pictures with the Castle in the background, we wandered down Main Street, and over to our left to Adventure Land. We took Helen on the Jungle Ride boat where she screeched at being attacked by the crocodiles with their mouths open showing all their sharp teeth. She jumped back when the rhinos poked their horns at the boat, and the elephants reared up and roared as we rounded a bend in the river.

We all went up in the Tree House to look out over the old wooden buildings that made up the street in Adventure Land. The Tiki-Tiki Room was a hit with its singing birds and catchy tune. As we continued around, we joined the line that wound around the popular "It's a Small World" pavilion. We finally boarded the small boat and Helen's little head pirouetted from side to side as she tried to take in each doll singing in their native tongue. She was so excited to see and hear the Russian doll I thought she would jump right out of the seat!

We all enjoyed most of the rides all together, but Jim took Helen on the Space Mountain roller coaster while I had Stassya drive one of the Autopia cars. She chose a blue one.

The new driver, on the right, headed out on the track.

There were two lines forming on the platform. We took the right side where a blue car was waiting. Stassya started to climb into the passenger seat, but I beat her to it and indicated that she was to be the driver. She had never driven a car before and didn't realize that she was on a track. I didn't bother to tell her and, as she weaved and bumped from side to side, I laughed until I cried. Stassya, on the other hand was very serious and very worried that she would crash the car and drove as if her life depended on it. She couldn't control the gas pedal and didn't know that it would suddenly slow the car when she lifted her foot. So besides weaving, we bumped and jerked all around the track. Stassya was a bit mad at me when we finished, for laughing at her, until I pointed out that she was actually on a track. We had a good laugh together over that, and I teased her unmercifully while she would pout, with a twinkle in her eyes.

I could not convince Jim or Stassya to come on my favorite Tea Cup ride with me, both claiming they would get dizzy and nauseous, but Helen was game. We picked out a pretty pink cup with a large dark rose-colored heart painted on the side.

The Tea Cup Ride at Disneyland

After I showed Helen how to twirl the cup with the wheel in the middle between us, we whirled madly around in circles, and then we staggered off at the end of the ride, dizzy, holding on to each other, and laughing like two crazy, drunken girls. It was times like these that I realized we did not have a language barrier at all. Both days ended with the magical evening fireworks over Sleeping Beauty's castle.

The following day, we said our goodbyes to Florence and Lady and started our long drive home. On the way, Jim stopped at a fruit stand so we could buy some oranges to eat fresh off the tree. There was a large grove of orange trees right next to the road. Jim took pictures of Stassya and Helen hugging the trees while I bought four large, juicy oranges.

As we climbed back into the car, Stassya asked me why I didn't buy the whole box. I remembered then, the stash of bananas I had seen in Leningrad at the home of one of the host families. It reminded me that Stassya had told me when you saw something good and precious in Russia, you bought as much as you could. Stassya told us that she could only find one orange in the last days before she left Leningrad to come and stay with us, and she had cut it in half, given one piece to Helen and the other to Paul. She had then made herself a cup of tea and left the room, so that she wouldn't have to watch them eat the sweet, juicy orange. She told me even much later in our friendship, that tea was just about all she had in those last few days before she came to us. I realized that I still had a lot to learn about my new friend.

We drove home singing "It's a Small World After All" over and over and over. For me it had more meaning than ever before.

22. The Holiday Season

This year's Thanksgiving dinner was to be at our house. To prepare, I explained our family traditions to Stassya, and then I poured over my traditional dinner items, and made a list. Since I was providing the turkey, my mother offered to bring her specialty: candied yams with marshmallows melted over the top. Our oldest son Andrew and his wife Dianne traditionally spent Thanksgiving with Dianne's family. Our younger son David and his wife Katrina lived in Colorado at this time. We would not see them until Christmas. Our daughter Joelle and her husband Mike lived nearby. They offered to bring a green salad and a vegetable. Stassya decided that she would like to bake an apple pie just the way Florence had taught her, so off we went to the grocery store.

"Let's get the biggest one!" Stassya said, as she stood looking into the bin of fresh-frozen turkeys. I showed her how to read the weights on the labels and told her to go for it! She pawed around, until she found the largest one and, with a heave and a wide grin, she plunked it into the cart.

"I can make soup with the bones," Stassya declared.

"Yes, you can," I happily responded, as I pushed the cart towards the produce department. *Oh boy*, I thought. *I will be so happy to have you make my soup.*

It didn't take Stassya long to get acquainted with our grocery store, as she had tagged along with me every single time I went shopping. She was mastering sales coupons, checking and comparing prices, and loved using my debit card!

"Dahling, I can't believe you don't need any money when you shop," she would say every time we came to the cash register.

Nothing I could say would change her mind regarding using debit/credit cards instead of cash, and receiving cash out of the wall at the ATM machine. To her, everything seemed to be free for the taking. There were so many things I took for granted. *This one calls for a lesson later about our banking system,* I thought.

The day before Thanksgiving, I gave Stassya free reign in my kitchen. I tied one of my aprons around her waist and left the room. She was so happy you could hear her singing and humming as she banged among the pots and pans and utensils. She was chopping apples like mad, rolling out the crust, and slapping it into shape with great enthusiasm. I couldn't watch, and kept out of her way. The kitchen began to smell heavenly, and the finished pie was twice the height as what mine would have been. It was a picture-perfect success, but the kitchen was a mess! Apple cores and skins were everywhere. Flour dusted the counter and everything on it. I gave the cook a cup of tea and cleaned it all up before I joined her to admire her handiwork sitting before us in the middle of the table.

Thanksgiving Day arrived. We were up very early to prepare the turkey for the oven. We set the table with my finest white china decorated with pink flowers around the rim. The tablecloth was a matching pink, and the burgundy cloth napkins, folded by Helen and draped over the rims of the pink Russian wine and water glasses I had purchased in Helsinki about two years earlier completed the picture.

Finally, everyone had arrived, and we were all assembled in our finery. Everything was ready to put on the table. Stassya and Helen posed for a picture with the table decoration they had made, a large pineapple which graced the center of one of my glass cake platters. The pineapple was surrounded with oranges, apples, and grapes.

Our Thanksgiving table decoration

It made a pretty picture with tall candles lit on each side. Dinner was a great success, but the dessert of apple pie with a scoop of vanilla ice cream on top was clearly the favorite. We finished every bite and wished for more. (It remains my favorite request of Stassya to this day.)

Christmas was quickly arriving on the back of Thanksgiving. I planned to have an Advent calendar for Helen. For Joelle's first Christmas, my father had made an eighteen-inch tall, flat, wooden Christmas tree with a star on top. He painted it a dark green and screwed twenty-four small golden hooks on the surface on which my mother and I had hung little gifts. This was a practice we continued until Joelle was grown and had left home. Even now, I give her seven gifts to be opened, one on each of the seven days before Christmas. I also do it during the week before her birthday in April. My mother still does the same, along with a cake for both myself and for my sister Kay on our birthdays.

I hung this treasured tree for Helen from the mantle over our fireplace and attached twenty-four gift tags of different designs with ribbon, one on each hook. On each tag I had written a number. I then purchased twenty-four small-to-medium gifts, wrapped them in an assortment of last years' leftover Christmas paper and bows and put them in a basket on the hearth below the Advent tree.

Twenty-four days until Christmas

Every day of December, Helen was to choose one tag, untie it from the tree, and find the matching number on one of the packages. She was up very early every morning. She would quietly tiptoe out to the living room, dig carefully in the basket, find the matching number, and open one package. Like her mother the year before, she smoothed the wrapping paper, placed the bow on top, and left it on the hearth for future use. She would put her little gift next to her placemat on the dining table and would reach over and touch it during breakfast. One day it was a pair of socks with Santa on them, another was a finger puppet, and yet another, a set of colored pencils, or sometimes a tasty holiday treat and so forth. I had as much fun picking them out as she was having opening them!

Joy on the first day of December!

On the first Saturday in December, Joelle and Mike went with the four of us to the Christmas tree farm where we had to choose the one perfect tree out of hundreds. This was usually Jim's job. Every year, early in December, he would park our oldest son Andrew at one tree he thought would be "the one", and then go off between the trees and spy another possibility. He would park our other son David at that one and off he would disappear into another row of trees. This went on with Joelle left standing next to a third tree, and then me at a fourth. When I would finally say I'd had enough, he would reluctantly select another tree, not one of the ones we were each holding onto, but a completely different one, claiming it was the tallest and most beautifully formed. (Many years later, only Joelle would go with him to the tree lot.)

In 1977, we had just moved into our new four-bedroom home, and, except for a sofa, we had not yet furnished our large living room. So I did not object when Jim picked out absolutely the largest tree on the lot. We arrived home with a tree on top of the car, hanging over the front and back of our large station wagon. We all helped to carry the tree into the house. When we laid it down across the floor to put the stand on it, it stretched diagonally from the front door, through the living room, and into the dining room! Upon standing it up, I was not surprised to see that it was taller than our eighteen-foot ceiling. Down it came again, a bit was chopped off at the bottom, remounted, and finally stood nearly touching the ceiling. The challenge of decorating it was daunting, but with a step ladder we managed to decorate it almost up to the top. Then Jim leaned over the railing of the stairs to the second story, reached out, and was able to put the angel on top—tilted a bit—but on the whole, the tree was beautiful, if a bit overdone.

One day, soon after we had finished our decorating, the priest from our new neighborhood church stopped by for a visit. I was embarrassed by our monster Rockefeller Center store-sized tree. Not only was it tall, but it stuck way out into the room. I was afraid it might appear overwhelming and garish, and apologized, but the priest assured me that it was beautiful and perhaps the largest decorated Christmas tree he had ever seen in someone's home!

So, this year, I made the suggestion that we give Helen the task of finding our tree. Jim grumbled just a little but gave in. I asked Helen what shape the tree should be. She showed us with her fingers that it should be wide at the bottom and pointed at the top.

The tree should be shaped like this...

Jim took pictures of this and of Helen peeking around the branches of the one she had finally chosen. It was the tallest and most perfect of all the trees, just as if Jim had trained her. As Jim, Stassya and I watched, Mike, Joelle and Helen proceeded to saw away at the trunk until the tree came down. After much effort, we tied the tree to the top of our car and drove home.

That Sunday, we took all our decorations from storage and loaded the tree with ornaments, bows, tinsel, rows of beads, and a beautiful porcelain angel on the top. Gifts, large and small, colorfully wrapped in red, silver, gold, and green with ribbons and bows attached, were appearing under the tree every day. Stassya and Helen would get down on their knees and peek at the name tags of each new one that appeared. Excitement was building....

I gave Helen the task of setting up our manger. On Jim's and my first Christmas together, Jim's grandfather Poppy made us a wooden manger about eighteen inches by eight inches, with an open front, two sides with windows, a roof over the top, and a small platform on the rooftop on which to place an angel. I had purchased a set of manger figurines at the dime store in 1962, and still had them. Jim back then had asked for some clean straw at a local farm, and we had glued some of the straw to the roof, storing the rest in a brown paper bag and using it to scatter throughout the inside of the manger.

I opened the storage box for Helen, took out the bag of straw, and spread the figurines out onto the floor. I put the manger on a small stool covered with a red cloth. Helen knelt down, and slowly and carefully arranged the holy family, the shepherds, wise men, camel, two sheep, and the donkey inside. Two white fluffy doves, one in each window, completed the inside picture. The angel with golden wings, dressed in a pink gown, was placed on the top. I plugged in the cord and the small light on the inside ceiling turned on to highlight the baby in the manager. Helen had the job of turning the light off at bedtime, and turning it back on in the morning. She would carefully check the next day to be sure everything was arranged just so, moving the clay figurines slightly, and speaking to them in a hushed whisper. It sounded as if she was gently scolding them for moving around during the night.

Helen in charge of the Christmas manger

When it was finally time to visit Santa at the mall, Stassya helped Helen put on a white blouse to go with the lace-edged red skirt she had made. Stassya tied Helen's hair back into a pony tail with a red and white bow. Jim took a picture of Helen on Santa's knee with her head cocked next to Santa's head. Her smile and glowing eyes lit up the picture. She seemed to be savoring every moment. If Helen spoke to Santa, it was in Russian. I assume he speaks the language of every child and, so therefore, would have understood Helen's request.

Helen's chat with Santa

One of the traditions I had begun with our three children was to bake Christmas cookies, and now I had a chance to teach Helen about rolling out the dough, cutting out shapes with the long-unused cookie cutters which had been stored in the back of one of my cabinets. There was a star, an angel, a gingerbread man, and a tree. After a short demonstration, Helen grasped the knack of rolling out the dough evenly with my rolling pin. She carefully chose one after another of the cookie cutters and pressed them down with the heel of her hand. We placed them on the baking sheet, and I put them in the oven. Meanwhile, Helen, with my help, measured out the frosting ingredients, mixed them up, and divided them into three bowls. One bowl of frosting we left white, and the other two we blended with color and created a nice dark red frosting for the gingerbread men, with a leafy green color for the trees. Lastly, I put out the sugar sprinkles in various colors, some mini chocolate chips for the eyes of the gingerbread men, and some little silver candy beads for the tree decorations. Stassya was our eager assistant, collecting our ingredients, washing used utensils, and putting things away. She was also our interpreter.

"Are they ready yet?" Helen asked as she peeked into the glass oven door. I had left the light on, so she could watch her cookies as

126

they baked. I wound up the timer and gave it to her to hold. It seemed as if the minutes ticked by very slowly, as Helen watched first the timer and then would go check on the cookies. The smell was heavenly and soon the first batch was ready to come out. We set them out to cool and put another batch into the oven.

When the cookies were cool and ready for decorating, I showed Helen what to do and left her on her own to create her pieces of art. Stassya and I sat down with a cup of tea and had a taste of a second and third cookie from the first batch—the first cookie chosen by Helen was her reward for a job well done.

Early on Christmas Eve, we had the whole family over, including Florence, who had flown in to visit, my mother Betty, Andrew, his wife Dianne, and their newest additions to our family, twins James and Alanna, by then five months old. David and his wife Katrina who had come in from Colorado, and Joelle and her husband Mike completed our family and filled our small home with chatter, laughter, and lots of cooing at the new additions.

Stassya had asked if she and Helen could play some Christmas songs on our piano before we started the festivities. They had been practicing for two weeks. Everyone gathered around the Christmas tree as Jim dimmed the lights. The twinkling lights on the tree reflected on the tinsel. The fireplace logs crackled and candles flickered on the mantel. Wrapped gifts were stacked about three feet high around the tree and spilled into the room. Helen began to sing "Silent Night, Holy Night" in English.

My family had never heard Helen sing as Jim, Joelle and I had in Leningrad when she had sung "My Bonnie Lies over the Ocean" at our student farewell party with the same effect. We were all quiet, some of us with tears in our eyes. It was a magical moment. Then Stassya and Helen broke the spell and lightened the mood by playing "Jingle Bells" and "Frosty the Snowman" together on the piano. Everyone sang along, making it the perfect beginning to our family Christmas Eve.

Playing Christmas songs.

We started with a light supper of Stassya's homemade turkey soup, cornbread, salad, apple cider, and, of course, for dessert, Stassya's apple pies. Florence gave Stassya a nod of approval, as she took her first bite. And when her plate was empty, Florence declared with a grin on her face, "You have surpassed my teaching. Well done!"

Finally while Joelle and Helen were on their knees scooting around the Christmas tree, checking all the tags, Jim was chosen to be Santa. His rules were very strict. "Only one gift at a time," Jim announced in a firm, no nonsense voice. "We all watch the unwrapping, admire the gift, and acknowledge the giver."

There was a hushed groan coming from somewhere in the room. I concluded that it was probably Dianne, as her family gave out all the gifts, piled them in front of the receiver and all members of her large family would open everything at once, making it utter chaos, but keeping the process to a reasonable time. On the other hand, Jim's ceremony of ours could last for many hours! Then, Jim finally called for a break.

Hot chocolate was ready as was a large plate of Helen's Christmas cookies, but Jim soon ordered us back to finish his task. Along with their gifts, Helen and Stassya each had a large stack of

128

perfectly smoothed out Christmas wrappings with a pile of bows on top. Andrew and David playfully took the rest of the torn and crunched paper, balled it up, and threw it into a plastic garbage bag. As the guys stated that we were finally finished, Stassya and Helen grabbed their stack of wrappings and bows, held tightly onto it while they crept out of the living room, and hid it in their closet along with all their other collections, which included among other like-items, zip plastic bags, and empty shampoo bottles.

After everyone left, the five of us, including Florence, heaved a sigh, and relaxed while Helen checked out her presents once again. We all hung our stockings on the fireplace with care, checked to see that the fire was out, set out a glass of milk and two cookies for Santa, and went to bed.

Christmas Day arrived before dawn with Helen creeping out of her bedroom. She discovered to her delight that the milk was gone and only crumbs were left of the cookies. There was a very large box in front of the fireplace with her name on it. She tiptoed back into her bedroom and woke up her mother. Of course, with all the creeping about and the whispering, Jim and I awoke. We joined the creepers downstairs and snuggled up on the sofa. Jim had turned on the Christmas tree lights, lit the fireplace, put on the coffee pot, and then we watched as Helen opened her box with the very large red bow on top from Santa. She squealed when she saw a perfect replica of a puppet theater complete with a king, queen, princess, ogre, and prince. We enjoyed our first of many puppet shows, this one in Russian and translated by Stassya, with the puppet princess singing "Silent Night, Holy Night" in perfect English! We all enjoyed opening our stocking gifts before having pumpkin-pecan waffles for breakfast.

23. Jim vs. the Cabbages

April 12th marked the end of Stassya's six- month visitor's visa. That date was coming up in one month. None of us could believe the last five months had passed so quickly! While sitting at our dining room table after a meal one evening, the three of us were talking back and forth. That was when I happened to notice that Helen, sitting next to me, was paying close attention.

"She knows what we are saying!" I looked at her with a smile and threw her a kiss. Helen looked at me with a knowing grin from ear to ear.

"We'll have to be careful what we say from now on," I teased.

"Yes," Helen replied with a nod of her head.

The next day I approached Stassya regarding extending her visa.

"Stassya," I began, as we were drinking our afternoon cup of tea. "I have a suggestion to make." I was unsure how to approach this topic without begging on my hands and knees, so I dove right in.

"How about extending your visa to let Helen finish her school year?" I held up my hand indicating that I wanted to continue before Stassya said anything. "I know you can extend it, but I'm not sure if it is three months or six. I think even by three months' time Helen would be speaking English with some proficiency. Just think what that would do for her at her school in Leningrad." From experience, I knew that understanding a language came before speaking, but that speaking comes rapidly after that. Besides, I was not yet ready to let my friend go. I held my breath.

"It's funny you should say that," Stassya said. "I've been thinking about that, too."

Thank goodness, I thought. *I really don't want to pass out while*

130

I am waiting for an answer, please say yes.

"I think it is a good idea, but I am worried about my job. Not for me," she said with a sigh, "but for my students. I feel responsible for them. And, Paul, what would he think, and what would happen when I return home after nine months or even a year?" This was said with a catch in her throat.

We discussed these and other problems that might come with an extended stay, such as Helen returning to her class in Leningrad and to the reality of Russia at the moment—the lack of adequate food and the breakdown of society such as they had known. We had many midnight talks and, during this time, Stassya also sadly confided to me that her relationship with Paul was not very good.

Finally, Stassya made the decision to apply for the extension, but with the understanding that she and Helen would be leaving soon after school was out. Stassya applied, and before long had the extension that would allow Helen to finish her year, and I secretly hoped that it would take us through summer before they had to return to Russia.

In April, Helen was selected "Student of the Week". Her school year ended with her speaking English rather well, with excellent grades, and a very best friend, Debbie. Helen joined Debbie's Girl Scout troop, sold Girl Scout cookies door to door with great success, and went off to Girl Scout camp for one week. In eight months, she had adjusted completely and now had bloom in her cheeks, a happy smile, and lots of confidence.

Our student of the week!

Much to my relief, as I really do not enjoy cooking that much, Stassya had begun to take over some of that task for me. We had lots of borsht (beet soup), and cooked cabbage, pork, and potatoes with lots of garlic sauce. These were the ingredients she was used to preparing, especially during the long winter months in Russia when the summer produce was not available.

Stassya had been walking to the grocery store not far from our home to purchase the items she needed for the meals she cooked for us. One day she came home with a large shopping bag filled with cabbages.

"Dahlings, they were on sale so I bought lots of them," she announced in the kitchen.

"Not more cabbages," Jim complained. He had happened to walk into the room and when he spied the large bag of cabbages— not his favorite vegetable—he couldn't help himself from blurting out.

I saw the hurt look on Stassya's face and the tears starting down her cheeks, as Jim walked out of the kitchen. I followed him up the stairs and angrily told him either he could eat every one of those cabbages or he could pack his bags and move out, and before he did that he had better make amends with Stassya.

It all turned out okay, with Jim's apology to her, a big hug, and his promise to eat every bite she put on his plate. From then on, Stassya would sneak into the house and hide her purchase of sale items outside under the overhang on her deck, particularly cabbages. I didn't even know she was doing this until I happened to spy the shopping bag one day sitting outside the sliding door to her bedroom. We had a good laugh over that...which leads me to another episode which made Jim eat his words.

Helen's school was planning on having their annual silent auction fundraiser. Stassya came to me with an idea to participate. The school personnel, teachers, and students had taken Helen under their wings and made her feel so welcome that Stassya wanted to say thank you. Her idea was to offer a Russian evening in someone's home, which would include a Russian meal cooked and catered for six, and an hour of Russian stories and music. I helped her write up the flyer which would be put on a table describing in colorful detail what would be offered: *piroshkies* (little pie crust fold-overs with a filling of ground beef and cabbage), two of my favorite Russian salads—one a tangy beet salad and a delicious cabbage slaw. She had to include her borsht soup and her entree signature dish of pork, potatoes, cabbage, and garlic sauce. For dessert: American apple pie baked by a Russian.

"No one is ever going to bid on that," Jim said quietly to me with conviction one day after seeing the menu.

We all attended the evening of the auction held in the school's large multi-purpose room and a small room off on the side. A large crowd of parents attended, and we joined them wandering around the two rooms, looking at all the nice offerings. We also placed our bids on a couple of interesting items.

As it was getting near the end of the bidding time, excitement was building—particularly in a back corner of the small room. There was loud bidding going on right up to the last second. We tried peering over and around the people stacked up around one spot on the table. Then the bidding bell rang. Loud yelling, clapping, and laughter erupted. The crowd finally thinned out, so that we could see what all the hoopla was about and found that it was Stassya's flyer! Jim was bowled over when he saw the final bid for Stassya's cabbage dinner and entertainment. At $470, it was the highest bid of the entire auction! Stassya poked Jim and gave him a coy smile.

"Congratulations, my dahling," he said with a chuckle, as he hugged her. "You just outdid yourself."

The winners of the bid were two couples, friends, who wanted to have a grownups' evening with Stassya. They hired babysitters at one of their homes, and eagerly awaited Stassya at the other couple's home. Stassya and I arrived, carrying all the prepared food in an ice chest, and some Russian table decorations, pictures, and music CDs in a box. I helped Stassya set the table and make the final preparations, while the two couples had some wine and ate every single *piroshky* for an appetizer. We were soon ready and called them to dinner. Stassya served the couples, describing each item as she placed it on their plates. Every morsel was eaten with enthusiastic compliments. Before we finally served and joined them for dessert, Stassya sat on a stool and entertained them with her stories and some Russian music, while I cleaned up the kitchen. The evening was very successful and we drove home, two happy caterers with an empty ice chest. Jim now realized the value of Stassya's cooking and never complained again.

AN EVENING IN RUSSIA COPY   C338

Dinner and Armchair Travel
by Stanislava Nazarova

* Dinner for 6 served in your home.
* Borsch and other Russian dishes are on your menu.
* Dinner will be cooked, served and cleaned up.
* Invite 2 other couples or your own family.
* After dinner you will travel among the great palaces
  and museums of St. Petersburg, learn of its incredible
  history and appreciate the bravery and courage of its
  people through the slides and narrative of
  Mrs. Na

Stanislava Nazarova

SPRING FOR OUR KIDS

Item # C338   Value $ Priceless

Section # C   Minimum Raise $ 2.00

Description "An Evening In Russia"

NUMBER	BID
Starting Bid	10.00
Jack Blades	20.00
Dottie Blades	22.00
Bob + Joan Murphy	24.00
2 Ammboce	26.-
Nancy Fox	30.00
J. Marke	60 —
Sue Christie	65 -
Jim Katon	150.00
J. Blades	200.00
J. Katon	300.00
M. Blades	310.00
J. Katon	400.00
M. Blades	450
J. Katon	470
Reed	

The Silent Auction bid: An Evening in Russia
Value: Priceless!

24. A Big Decision to Make

Without giving any thought to a realistic future, I began to come up with a plan to approach Stassya about staying in the USA permanently. I didn't want to push her into it, but wanted to let her know she had the option, in case she was thinking along those same lines. It would mean that she would have to abandon her mother, sister, husband, job, friends, and her possessions back in Russia. It could mean that she might never be able to go back. It would mean leaving the country she loved, and everything that was familiar. It would mean denying Helen her father, and her beloved grandmother Sophia, and Freddy the fox which we had sent her for a gift, along with any other treasures Helen had collected. It would mean that Helen would grow up as an American, not a Russian, and could probably eventually lose most of her Russian language.

These thoughts almost made me give up; but on the other hand, I weighed all of it with the conditions I saw in Russia and the letters Stassya had written me when she was there about the most current conditions.

Why not give them a chance at a better life? I thought. *How can I send them back without at least offering them a choice? Am I being selfish?* My thoughts were going in circles. *What would Jim say? What would be our responsibilities? How can we keep them here in our little home with almost no privacy for Helen as she gets older?* The questions kept coming. Finally, I put this idea and these questions to Jim.

"How can we not give her the choice," Jim countered. "Besides, making the offer gives her both sides. Tell her exactly what you just told me." We were both silent for a moment before Jim continued.

"Stassya is a very intelligent, responsible woman. She does not hide from reality." Again a moment of silent thought. "She has not and would not avoid her responsibility to Helen or to anyone else depending on her. We both know that she is capable of making the best decision for both of them."

"I know, but look what she has to give up," I said. "Can I ask her to do that?" I slumped down in my comfortable chair, in my comfortable home, thinking about always having plenty of food in my refrigerator.

"Yes, you must at least ask her." Jim replied firmly. "If you don't, you will always regret just sending her back."

Late that night, I lay awake long after the lights were out, then finally got up, tiptoed downstairs so as not to wake anyone, took a blanket off the back of the upstairs sofa, my pillow, and a good book to distract me, and headed to the living room sofa. I turned on the table lamp, lay down, and stared at the ceiling. My book remained closed, but my eyes remained open. I could not stop my thoughts.

It wasn't long before Stassya stepped into the room and joined me. She sat on the floor next to me.

"I saw the light on," she said quietly. "What is wrong, Gaylochka?" she asked with such concern in her voice.

"I am thinking of you," I said as I sat up and looked at her. "I am worried about you and Helen going back to Russia."

"I am worried, too, but I think I have to go," Stassya said with a sadness I had never heard before. "I cannot bear to leave you, but what am I to do?"

We were both crying by that time. I was afraid Jim would hear us and wake up. He had to go to work early in the morning, so I wiped my tears and suggested a cup of tea. Daily, and usually more than once a day, we used this method to talk, plan, reminisce, console, and laugh. Even though it was late, I put out a little snack of cheese and apples. We looked at each other, munched on our snack, drank our tea, exchanged a few quiet words without addressing the topic which now was on both our minds, and then headed back to our beds. I had opened the subject and knew we needed to continue exchanging our thoughts another time very soon.

And soon it was….

"My dear Gayle," Stassya began as she wiped her hands on my drying towel. We were cleaning up the kitchen from breakfast the next morning, she washing, me drying. "How can I leave my

136

Motherland?" Stassya continued thoughtfully. "What will happen to my mother? It's too hard."

"I know," I answered. "Those questions have kept me awake at night. I can't answer them for you. I can only listen as you work through to a decision."

With that the subject was dropped, and I grabbed the car keys as we dashed out the door to take Helen to school. We had work to do in my office, so we did not talk again until our evening cup of tea at the dining room table.

"What do I do about Paul, my apartment, my books and piano? I could never go back, you know," Stassya was continuing our conversation as if we had never stopped talking that morning. "And how would I find a job to support myself and Helen?" she asked. "I could not live with you forever, Gayleochka. It would not be fair."

She's right, I thought, *I have no idea how it would work.* The questions stopped for a few days. I could see the struggle Stassya was having. She was quiet and had a far-away look in her eyes, and she spent a lot of time in her room or out on the upstairs deck, sleeping in the warm sun.

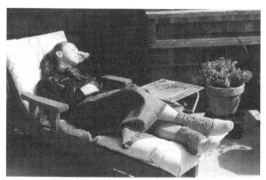

Time off from making a life-changing decision

The next question came out of the blue one day while we were collating some materials for a student group.

"If I stay, how to do it?" Stassya asked me. We always seemed to be on the same thought wave.

"I don't know," I answered her. I was trying very hard to keep from jumping up and down with joy, but in my mind I was saying: *Maybe, oh I hope so, yes, yes, yes.* My thoughts tumbled around in my head. Then I sobered up, kept a straight face as best I could, turned around, and walked out of the room. When I was out of sight, I high-fived myself, put two thumbs up, and if I could have, I would have jumped high and clicked my heels together. Of course, it was only a question, but it was a start!

Meanwhile, Stassya and I told Jane, a Russian friend and neighbor, what we were thinking about doing. To start with, Jane gave me the name of a local lawyer who handled these kinds of cases. I called for an appointment.

"We have an appointment with the lawyer here in town," I announced to Stassya the next morning. "It is for information only, a free consultation." I could see the anxiety in her face, especially knowing of her great fear of approaching any official. Even to make an exchange at JC Penney or to open a small bank account sent her into great anxiety. A policeman would probably cause her to faint. Now being asked to go to the office of a lawyer and actually speak to him about her personal situation was probably too much. Stassya nodded and left the room.

That afternoon, both of us intimidated, we walked into the lawyer's office. He was friendly and seemed knowledgeable. He outlined the process which included reams of forms, and the need for a documented story of the reason for applying for refugee status. The lawyer pointed out that being a refugee means that one has a fear that on returning to one's country, there is a chance you could be watched, be picked up, harassed, and/or imprisoned.

"How much would this cost?" I asked him.

"We would start with a retainer plus the cost of filing," the lawyer answered. "Then it depends on how smooth a process it is, or how complicated. And there is an hourly rate."

"Thank you very much," I replied as I stood up. "We'll get back to you as soon as we are ready." Stassya and I shook his hand, smiled pleasantly, and turned to leave the office. As we silently walked to my parked car, I sighed. I knew the amounts he had in mind would be too high.

"I can't pay that amount of money, and I won't let you do it," Stassya stated firmly.

"Never mind using a lawyer," I said. "We can do this ourselves." I couldn't think how at the moment, but I was determined to find out.

"Well, I have a story," Stassya said quietly.

"You what?" I said as I stopped, startled, and turned to her. I wasn't sure I had heard her correctly so I said again, "What did you just say?"

"I have a story," Stassya repeated, louder this time and with conviction in her voice.

"Okay, let's stop here for an ice cream," I replied, as I saw the gelato counter in the window of La Vera's Pizza across the street. "I need to hear this…right now!" We each chose our favorite flavors in a cone and sat outside at a table in the warm sun. We licked at our cones, Stassya slowly and carefully, me fast to avoid the constant drips of its melting. Stassya seemed to be collecting her thoughts as she savored each bite. So I waited until she finished and watched as she carefully wiped her mouth.

"Okay, I'm waiting," I said, leaning forward so as not to miss a word, "Let's hear it."

25. Stassya's Family Story

"Gayle, dahling," she began. "It is difficult to know where to start, but I will tell you what I know."

"Tell me. I will help you with the details later," I said, trying not to sound too excited.

"I had a grandfather I never knew, and an uncle, the older brother of my father. You know, Gaylochka, that I have Polish blood in my family."

If she had told me this before, I didn't remember. I shrugged, shook my head, and waited for her to continue.

"They came from what you know as Poland, near Krakow, and settled in Krasnadov in Southern Russia," she said.

I was trying hard to be patient. I just nodded.

"You know the nice Russian coat I had made for you?" she went on.

I nodded again.

"One of the women in the family made it for you," she said. "That is her business."

(The Russian coat she had given me was an exact replica of the one Stassya had, black nylon, with a very warm, down lining. It zips from the chin all the way down the front and ties at the waist. It is ankle length. It is not used very often in California, but we have traveled in the winter to Switzerland, Canada, and to Colorado where I was able to use it. I am very grateful for that warm, soft garment when it is needed, plus its softness allows me to fold it up into a small bundle for ease of packing.)

Stassya had stopped for a moment, and then continued. It sounded to me as though she was revisiting her own memories not just those of her ancestors, and her voice sounded far off. It gave me the shivers.

"My grandparents and their family left Krakow in 1914 when World War I began," she went on. "They moved east into Russia where they felt safer. They were of noble origin and owned some land and a leather factory there. Then the Russian Revolution started. The land was confiscated and only the factory remained with no workers left, only the family members. They no longer felt safe in Russia, but they could not go back to Krakow. The revolutionary fighting among the Russians, and also the war raging all over Europe made it impossible. Then, in 1937, during Stalin's purges, the two oldest men in the family were arrested—my grandfather and his oldest son, my uncle. They disappeared along with millions as we are now being told."

I leaned back in my chair, prepared for a long, sad story.

"The family doesn't know what happened," Stassya went on, "but they think someone exposed that my grandfather was Polish and owned a factory. They may have had a grudge or were jealous—this kind of thing happened during these years. The family was scared, because when someone in the family was arrested, usually the wife and children soon followed, and they could be separated for the rest of their lives."

This is heavy, I thought. *Maybe we should go and continue this when we get home.* But Stassya was on a roll, and hardly took a breath before she continued.

"The wife of my uncle, my aunt, had been out with her daughter and was returning home one day in 1937 when a neighbor saw her and motioned to her. The neighbor whispered to my aunt that her husband and his father had been taken away by the authorities while she was out. My aunt immediately took her daughter, turned around, and with only the little money she had with her, went to the train station, bought two tickets and left. She had no documents or money."

"What happened to your grandmother?" I asked. "Didn't she leave, too?"

"No, my grandmother was too stubborn," said Stassya. "Her other two daughters, my father's sisters, were married with different names and lived close by—not in the same house. She figured they were safe, so she wasn't worried about them. And I guess my grandmother thought she could take care of herself, and wanted to be where my grandfather could find her when he returned."

141

"Well, where did your aunt and your cousin go? How did they exist without papers and money? Did they ever find out about what happened?"

"They took the train to Astrachan, and eventually, my aunt got a job in a hospital. She lived secretly for two years until she changed her last name and got new papers."

"Your uncle who disappeared, wasn't he your father's brother? What happened to your father?" I asked.

"My father left and went to Leningrad."

"Did your grandmother and aunt ever find out about what happened to their husbands?"

"Stalin died in 1953," said Stassya. "My grandmother died before she found out. My aunt did not find out anything until 1988."

"Over 50 years later?" I was stunned!

"She received an official paper saying the case was closed. After the deaths, the government found them 'not guilty'."

"Is that all? Did your aunt ever find out where they were or what happened to them?"

"No, to this day no one knows what happened to them or where they are buried. Many of us Russians are just now finding out about the realities of Stalin's reign," Stassya said slowly. "Millions of Russians just disappeared. Now we are being told that most of them were sent to Siberia where they were worked, starved and froze to death. Many Russians did not make the connection to Stalin; we believed it was the circumstances of a hard life or the war," Stassya continued. "Stalin won the war for us, so how could we believe he would be killing our own people?"

This information was being told to me from a Russian teacher who was just finding out first hand that not everything she was taught was the truth.

"Go on," I said with a lump in my throat. I was hurting for my fragile friend.

"Well," Stassya replied, "Now we are just beginning to find out in the news that the Russian army not the Nazis killed all those Polish people and buried them in the forest during World War II. A great many Russian people have scorned the Polish people, and the Jews, especially out in the rural areas. I don't know what their fate will be with all that is going on in Russia right now," Stassya went on.

I was even more stunned. This was even worse than I thought! Before me sat this lovely, kind, thoughtful woman who loved her country, the foundation of which was unraveling into a scary society. The people no longer seemed to trust each other, and some were becoming very money-hungry, grabbing and fighting over what food they could get. Many were buying on the black market, and were bargaining with the mafia.

"I have Polish ancestry even though I was born in Russia, speak Russian, and was educated and work in Russia," Stassya continued. "But, I teach English to Russian boys and girls, and I have traveled outside of Russian territory. I believe I could be a target for the KGB," Stassya said with tears running down her cheeks. "Why do you think the Berson's asked you to sponsor Sasha [their 17 year old son]? He is Jewish, so is Masha, and others in the group I brought to America. Elena [the vice principal] and her husband live in fear that someone may return; and will try to knock their door down again and threaten them, as they did in the past. They are Jewish. It may be the same for the Polish, too, I think."

"Wipe your tears," I told her in a shaky voice. "That is enough for now. Let's go home."

At the same time, I was thinking of what to do. Now it was my turn to be quiet and thoughtful. Finally, after a day or two at home, as if I were still at the outdoor table at Vera's eating my ice cream, I asked Stassya:

"Do you think you could get a copy of your aunt's notification letter?"

As if she had been in a continuing conversation with me, Stassya answered:

"I can write to my mother, ask her to contact my aunt, and see if this is possible. Maybe it could be faxed to us."

Well, that would be a miracle, I thought, *but worth a try.*

"Let's do it faster," I suggested, "Let's try to call your mother." *Sometimes miracles do happen,* I thought, *but let's help it along.*

"By the way," I pondered, you said you are Polish. Is your mother Polish, too?"

"Yes, half Polish and half Belarussian, but no one knows that. She conveniently lost her documents during the siege of Leningrad by the Nazis in 1941. She changed her last name and put herself as "Russian" on the new papers," Stassya admitted.

"So this was a worry even then," I thought out loud.

"Yes, and I was told not to mention to anyone that my father was Polish. My mother did not want anyone else to know about it, even though it was still officially on his papers."

143

Stassya's father, Vladislav Stanislavovich Golovnya
(Stassya was named after him: Stanislava Vladislavouna Golovnya)

By now it was the end of July, and we had one month to put this paperwork together and get it to the immigration office in San Francisco before Stassya's visitor visa date was up in mid-September. I wasn't sure if it was a miracle or if we helped it along, maybe a combination of both, but we received the documentation we needed by fax from Russia shortly after Stassya's call to her mother. I couldn't understand what was said, but Stassya told me her mother would contact her sister-in-law immediately.

(The fax machine, being new to both of us, always produced a feeling of wonder.

"Good luck, fax machine," was Stassya's usual comment, as we had begun to send faxes all over the world. She would blow the piece of paper a kiss and wave goodbye, as it moved through the machine. When the fax machine would start to make the usual noise preceding an incoming fax, we would stand there together, watching as it fell into the tray.

"Hello! And where are you from, my treasure?" Stassya would ask the faxed piece of paper, and then would thank the "useful machine".)

The day the information from Russia arrived was even more "wondrous" as Stassya would later exclaim to anyone who would listen.

With the letter from her aunt, we were able to put together a detailed story of what happened in Stassya's family in 1937. We described her fear of returning at this time with her eleven-year-old

144

daughter. She wrote of her worry of being persecuted for living in Russia, but not being a full-blooded Russian, and how the infighting going on in Russia at this time was very frightening to her.

We edited Stassya's story, read it over and over, finally typed it on the computer, and filled out all the forms. I could see Stassya take a deep breath, and with a slight hesitation, she picked up the pen and signed her life-changing commitment—Stanislava Nazarova. We were both silent, as I drove us to the post office. We kissed the envelope goodbye as we dropped it in the slot, and now the wait was filled with doubt and anxiety—and hope.

It wasn't long before we received a letter from the immigration office stating that the application was being reviewed, and that Stassya would be notified for an interview. Meanwhile according to the letter, until the process was completed, she could stay in America. There was a big sigh of relief from both of us, as our lives could now continue, at least temporarily, including a new school year for Helen.

At last Stassya received her appointment time at the immigration office near Market Street in San Francisco. I drove her there and waited for her in the waiting room along with several other people. Stassya was visibly shaking when her name was called. She looked as if she were going to the guillotine when she walked away from me. I may have looked the same. I know I was holding my breath one minute and fidgeting the next. It was taking so long that I got worried. *Was Stassya being grilled? Did they think she was lying?*

As the office door opened, I felt the blood draining from my face. Stassya started to come out, and then she turned around towards the woman behind her as if to say something more to her. When she turned back around, I could see she was smiling. *Maybe it went well,* I thought as I exhaled and smiled back.

"The lady was very nice," Stassya told me as she sat down next to me. She took my hand, patted it, and went on, "She asked me lots of questions."

"I suppose you 'started from the beginning', as usual," I teased.

"Of course, Gaylochka," was her reply with that twinkle in her eye I had seen before.

Charmed the lady, I bet, I thought to myself. *No wonder it took so long.*

Stassya went on, "She told me I would receive a letter with the time for another interview." With that, we both got up and left the immigration office.

An official letter arrived some weeks later. It requested that Stassya come for a second interview at the same office in San Francisco. Once again, I waited in the outer waiting room with dozens of other people. I was nervous and sweating, and when I looked around the room, I saw others who seemed nervous, too. That didn't help. *What happens if they say no? Do they deport someone immediately? What do we do then? Can we reapply? Maybe we should have paid that lawyer.* My thoughts were making a wreck of me.

When the door opened, I was nearly in tears. I almost collapsed with relief when I saw Stassya smiling and shaking the hand of the lady who had interviewed her the first time. Stassya came towards me holding up her paperwork.

"Gaylochka," she said in an excited voice. "I will have a Green Card. I can stay with you in America!"

"This calls for a really big celebration!" I managed to say as I cleared my throat.

"Let's go to Ghirardelli's."

Because Stassya no longer wanted to share with me, we ordered two of our usual Alcatraz sundaes. We cracked the hardened chocolate on the top, swirled our spoons around the fluffy cloud of whipped cream on the edge of our dishes, and dug in.

"The nice lady told me that this was the best application she had ever handled, and she was very pleased to welcome me," Stassya related to me as she slowly licked her spoon. I was nearly finished with my double sundae. Stassya noticed, and smiled as she leaned over her dish, wrapping one arm protectively around it. She went on talking with hardly a pause.

"She said she hoped that one day I would become an American citizen!" Stassya then straightened up with such pride I had no doubt that one day it would happen. Little did I know of the twists and turns our lives would take from that point forward.

26. The Divorce

During one of our midnight chats, when Stassya would find me on the living room sofa reading because I couldn't sleep, she began to tell me about her relationship with her husband Paul, and how it affected her life and that of Helen's. At this time, it seemed that many Russian men had no goals for which to aim, no upward mobility. Some hadn't had to work hard for personal gain, as many things, such as living quarters and food coupons, even though in spare quantities, were given to them by the government. Vodka was sold on every street corner out of kiosks, and the lines of men stretched down the sidewalks in all kinds of weather. Many of the men became alcoholics because of plentiful and cheap vodka, easy to come by with no questions asked.

"Sometimes, when Paul is very late, I go outside, even in the frozen winter, and look for him," Stassya confided with sadness in her voice. "Once I found him lying in the snow, passed out. I drug him inside, up in the elevator, into our apartment, and put him to bed."

"Nothing I try to do or say changes anything. You know," she went on great concern in her voice, "Paul sometimes frightens Helen. She usually asks me when we are in the bus on the way home from school, if her father is okay today. She has even looked up at our window before entering our apartment building; if the window is dark, that means he is not at home, and she will skip back to me with a happy face." Stassya hesitated then went on, "If the light is on in the window, she will come back to me with her head down and dragging her feet. That tells me he is home and will usually be drunk."

How can I respond to this? I thought. But, I took a chance:

"Have you thought that Paul could be an alcoholic?" I asked tentatively, as I had no experience with this condition.

"What exactly is that?" Stassya asked me with a puzzled look.

"Well," I said, "When a person becomes addicted, it can change his or her personality and they may begin to rely heavily on the alcohol. I understand that condition is considered a disease by the medical field." I stopped there in my explanation, as I could see that Stassya did not really understand what I was saying, perhaps it was the translation.

"I never considered it a disease," she said doubtfully. "I just thought it was a habit. Besides, he stopped drinking once when he had to take medication for forty days. Then he began to drink again."

"Well," I went on, "We have lots of treatment centers and support groups in this country to help such people and their families. Some do recover, but many struggle with this condition all their lives."

"Hmmm," she said and dropped the subject.

Around this time, Jim had two weeks of vacation coming, and he and I had discussed taking a cruise, so I looked around the internet for a cruise in Alaska. I found a good price on a seven-day cruise on the Island Princess, which would leave from the Anchorage port and end in Vancouver, B.C. I booked Jim and me on a flight to Fairbanks, a one-night hotel stay, and then the train from Fairbanks to Anchorage. Stassya was a bit worried about being in charge not only of our home, but of the Outbound Office of CHI, but I made sure everything was in order and left instructions for her to call the main office of CHI if anything came up with the students who were abroad. I knew she was capable and would do a good job. She was already doing my grocery shopping and cooking so I was not worried about meals. Jim and I left the house with full confidence and excitement for our first cruise.

When we arrived in Anchorage, we were met by the owners of the bed and breakfast I had reserved. Our accommodations were perfect, a lovely two-bedroom suite in the basement of the owner's home, which included a full kitchen stocked with breakfast items. It was still broad daylight outside at 10:00 p.m. the day we arrived, so we stepped out for a short walk and saw the next-door neighbor of the B & B on her knees gardening, which we found to be amazing at that hour of the night. We had a nice chat with her, and she indicated her surprise at how late it had gotten to be. The next morning, we were driven to the train station by our hosts where we boarded the train for a short ride to the coast, and then joined our cruise ship.

One evening during the cruise, Jim and I decided to go dancing after dinner. We had danced during our dating years, but it was the usual hug and sway of our high school years. We noticed several couples on the dance floor who were doing some fancy footwork, twirling and turning, so we sat out the rest of the dances, fascinated by their expertise. That night, I was looking through the daily activities guide for the next day. It was waiting for us on our bed when we returned to our cabin after dinner. There was a dance class offered in rhumba the next day at 2:00 in the afternoon. We made a note of the venue, and after lunch, headed to the lounge in the back of the ship.

There was a young staff member with one other person in the class. The "teacher" told us that she'd just learned the dance that morning from another staff member, but that it was not difficult. She would teach us the basic step and a turn. We were surprised at how easy it was, and enjoyed the last few minutes of the class dancing the rhumba to the music the teacher had put in the tape player.

We can do this! I thought to myself, and decided we would follow up on dance classes when we got home.

And what a greeting it was when we did arrive home! Sitting on the entry table were balloons, a vase of flowers, and a handmade *Welcome Home* sign drawn by Helen. Stassya had prepared homemade borsht soup, a lovely salad, and her now, signature apple pie. After dinner, Jim and I demonstrated our rhumba with lots of clapping and enthusiasm from Stassya and Helen.

"You are professionals, my dahlings," proclaimed Stassya. Jim bowed over Helen's hand, and asked her to dance the rhumba with him, much to her delight. We all laughed. It was so nice to be back home with our little family.

Soon after our return to Santa Rosa, Jim and I began our beginning ballroom dance lessons with John and Emily Ross at the Charles Schulz Ice Arena (of Snoopy fame). The classes were held upstairs where there was a very nice wood floor. The large inside windows overlooked the ice rink. The evenings we spent there were very festive and before long we were learning the waltz, foxtrot, and dancing the cha cha with the other beginners. (By now, as I write this, dancing has become a lifelong hobby for us. We have been taking lessons and going dancing on a regular basis now for over twenty-five years.) We soon had a chance to share our dancing with Stassya, and as it turned out, it changed her life as well.

On our first morning at home after our cruise, Stassya and I were having our cup of tea. She listened as I told her about our experiences in Alaska and on the ship. Just as I was about to pick up our cups and take them to the sink, Stassya signaled to me to sit back down.

"I have made a decision," she said in a serious voice.

Uh, oh, I thought. *I hope she hasn't decided to go back to Russia after all.* I remained quiet but I could feel the blood draining from my face, and my heart was beating fast. I dreaded to hear her next words. I think Stassya could tell that I was nervous and anticipating the worst, because she immediately put me at ease.

"Since I have decided not to go back to Russia," she began. I took a deep breath, swallowed, and relaxed, then she went on, "I've thought for a long time and also decided that I would get a divorce from Paul."

I was shocked! Maybe I shouldn't have been surprised, but I was totally unprepared for this statement.

"How would this be possible?" I asked her. "Would you have to go back to Russia to do this?"

"No, I don't have to go back," she reassured me. "I would have to fill out papers at the Consulate in San Francisco."

"Really? How do you know that?" I asked her. "That is all you have to do?"

"In Russia, my dahling," as she began another of her 'stories'. I set the tea kettle on the stove, grabbed two more tea bags, and sat back down. Stassya's stories took lots of time as she always started 'from the beginning'.

"I'm ready, tell me." She had my full attention, as usual.

"In Russia," she began again, "divorce is easy. You fill out the papers, it is done. Then you go home and live together forever."

"What do you mean, 'live together'?" I was puzzled.

"When you are given an apartment to live in by the government, that is yours for life—there is no other, even when you part company with your husband. You have no place to go." This she said with such finality.

"How does that work? What if everyone is angry and they hate

150

each other?" I asked with disbelief.

"It has to work. There is no other way. That's it." She went on, "Remember when I told you about our first apartment in Leningrad? Our bed was the only thing that fit into that little room. You had to climb over it to get from one side to the other. You had to sit on it to eat. All the families in the communal flat had to use the same kitchen, and the same toilet." She stopped talking as she took a sip of tea. I was aghast and nearly speechless, but I had a lot of questions:

"How did you keep the other people from eating your food?" I started. "The bathroom must have been awful!" This was beyond my imagination. I'm thinking, *This is what communism is? You share everything! You accept it and believe this is the best system?* I didn't say anything; I couldn't without becoming angry and perhaps saying things best left unsaid.

"I know what you are thinking, Gaylochka," Stassya said. "Some people did have trouble with food being stolen, but then they would put their refrigerator in their room or lock it with a chain I didn't have that kind of trouble because my mother-in-law lived in one flat, Paul's aunt in another, and a single woman who kept to herself lived in the fourth one. But there were constant fights and arguments between Paul, his mother, and his aunt. That is when he began to drink."

Stassya looked at me with such sadness at this point and then went on, "Paul and I went to the same school, so I knew him from childhood. He was handsome and very intelligent. He finished first in his college with a degree in mathematics and engineering. All of this changed when he began to drink. He was unpredictable, and soon I just wanted to escape with nowhere to go."

This was heavy stuff to me. I had never experienced any of this and did not know how to respond. Even though I was older by twelve years, I felt so unknowledgeable and naive. I listened; that seemed the best I could do. Then, to take the heaviness out of our conversation, I lightened it up a bit.

"Okay," I said, "then who cleaned the toilets?"

"Theoretically, you would take turns each week, but I ended up cleaning them all the time," Stassya said. "Let me explain about the flats," she went on. "First of all, many of them were palaces of the rich along Nevsky Prospect [the main street in Leningrad]. They had been confiscated by the communist government, and then divided up into little rooms with partitions and given to families."

By this time, the tea was cold, but Stassya took a sip and

continued with her story.

"When I became a teacher, I was on the list for a special apartment. It took many years, but you saw my nice apartment. It has a kitchen and a bathroom which I didn't have to share. I was one of the lucky ones. I painted it myself and put up the wallpaper. Now it will all become Paul's...lucky man."

"Whew," I gasped. This was almost too much for me to take in one sitting. "Let's get to work. I should check my office and see if I need to handle anything immediately."

"Don't worry," Stassya reassured me. "I have taken care of your office while you were gone. There is only one thing you need to do. Come, I'll show you." She stood up and took our cups to the sink.

I followed her out of the kitchen and up the stairs to my little office. I was still thinking about having to share my kitchen with other families, not just one or two people, whole families—and the bathroom, oh my, the filth, the smell...! When I was in Russia and on tours of the museums and palaces, I remembered the smell of the bathrooms. The smell reached way down the hall, even before you could see the door of the bathroom. I have already mentioned the toilet facility on the way to Novgorod where we had stopped with the bus. The women had all chosen to go out in the bushes rather than deal with the smell.

Since Stassya had told me that she could file for her divorce at the Russian Consulate, we decided on a day for our next trip to San Francisco. I dreaded going back to the Russian Consulate. I would not have wanted to confront that stoic, icy woman behind the glass window again. Thank goodness, that part would belong to Stassya this time. I drove across the Golden Gate Bridge, past the Presidio, and onto the lovely tree-lined street where the Consulate was located. I pointed out the white van, which was still sitting there, to Stassya.

"There is one just like it parked outside of the American Consulate in Leningrad," she commented. I was tempted to turn around and wave, but thought better of it, for Stassya's sake.

Up the wooden steps we went and waited at the door until it buzzed us in. This time I could sit and wait while Stassya conducted her business with the forms. She did not seem to be intimidated by the stern official at the window. Filing for the divorce was quick and easy. It wasn't long before we emerged from the Victorian house. After we got in the car we sat silently together for a few moments.

152

"It is done," Stassya said, as she heaved a sigh.

"Yes, I know," I acknowledged. "Do you want to celebrate or go home?" I asked her, unsure just how she was feeling at this moment.

"Definitely, a celebration," she enthused. "This calls for Ghirardelli's, don't you think?"

"Yes and double the chocolate!" I laughed as we drove off.

We were the first customers at the chocolate factory that morning. To my surprise, they no longer had the Alcatraz Sundae on the menu. I questioned the man taking our orders at the front of the shop. He told us to wait a moment and came back with another employee. This young man had been with Ghirardelli's for some time and knew about The Alcatraz. He promised to make it up for us with double the chocolate. It was simply more chocolate than even we could eat, but we could not bring ourselves to waste it. Luckily, I had a couple of snack-size plastic bags in my purse, so we took the remaining chocolate home to be eaten later with our tea. When we took it out to have our treat, however, it had turned to a liquid, ugly color. With regret, we threw it away....

27. Back to Normal Life

In the spring, Florence (Jim's mother) came to visit once again, and was amazed at Helen's progress in English since her visit at Christmas time.

"Hello, Helen," Florence enunciated slowly.

"Hello, Grandmother Florence. How is Lady?" [Florence's white poodle] Helen said with fluency.

"Ah ha, I see you are speaking English now," Florence acknowledged. "Lady is just fine. She is staying with her friend Bingo. I can see you are growing taller, too." She guided Helen over to the sofa for a chat.

One evening during Florence's visit, we were all sitting and talking at the dining room table after dinner when I noticed Helen busily folding her napkin. I made a motion to the others, and pointed to Helen. We stopped to watch for a moment before Helen looked at me and said,

"Auntie Gayle, your napkin looks like this."

I looked down and sure enough, Helen had folded hers to match mine, a crude imitation of an origami crane, which I had not even known I was doing.

"Grandmother Florence," Helen went on, as she crumpled her napkin in a ball and held it up for us to see, "You do this." Sure enough, she had that right.

"Momochka," Helen said as she began to tear her napkin into little pieces and stack them neatly, "You do this every night while you are talking."

Our little Helen was growing up and had become very observant.

Meanwhile, my office was becoming very busy with outbound student activity. I had another idea, however, about how to advertise it. I suggested to Tom and Lilka that I go to different areas of the United States and hold seminars with the Area Administrators regarding reaching out to the local schools and teachers about setting up Sister Schools with Japan. My office would do all the necessary work with the travel arrangements, collecting the money, setting up pre or post hotels and tours, and providing cultural materials for the groups. This program eventually became very popular and made our office busier than ever!

One of the trips I took was to Portland, Oregon. During the two days I was there, I was taken to an outdoor marketplace where, while shopping there, I saw the biggest potato you could imagine. It must have weighed two pounds and was as big as a child's football! I bought it for Helen because I knew how much she loved potatoes. I wrapped it up as a gift and gave it to her when I returned home. She was ecstatic, and much to our delight, after I baked it, she ate every bite at one meal!

Another trip was to Washington, DC, to greet four groups of Russian high school students, give them a tour, and set them on their way to their respective host schools and families. Stassya went with me to translate, if needed. CHI was the recipient of a grant from the U.S. government that Stassya and I had applied for. It was intended to bring four different high school groups from four regions of Russia for homestays in four areas of the United States.

While in Washington, DC, tours were planned for the Smithsonian Museums, the Capitol building, changing of the guards at Arlington Cemetery, and Mount Vernon. Stassya was, to our benefit, her usual excellent tour guide with her exceptional knowledge of our history. It was a very successful two days, and all too soon, we were back in the office at home.

Meanwhile, Stassya had offered to give a special piano recital at Helen's elementary school. The principal asked her how many students she would like to have attending.

"But, all of them, of course," was her reply, as if there were no other choice.

The classical music she played along with her comments and stories about the composers and their music captivated the children. I was sure some of them had never even heard classical music.

While all this was going on, Stassya was becoming concerned

about paying her own way, so one day, when she overheard the vice principal saying that she needed someone to come and clean her home, Stassya said she would like to have the job, as long as she could walk there. It so happened the woman did live close by the school, and so thus began what became a series of cleaning jobs Stassya used to supplement the income I was able to give her.

Also, the vice principal had a friend named Betsy who asked if she would recommend Stassya to her. Stassya turned Betsy down as she lived way outside the city, and Stassya did not want to ask me to drive her "everywhere". But Betsy called her back and made an interesting suggestion. She volunteered to pick Stassya and Helen up on Friday after school, and they could have dinner and spend the night with Betsy and her husband Dan. Betsy would then drive her back the next day. Thus began a close, long-lasting friendship full of laughter and fun. Stassya and Betsy would eventually work together as area coordinators for CHI, welcoming Japanese high school students and their teachers for short homestay visits just like the one Stassya had participated in, in 1989 with her Russian students.

It was at one of my semi-annual trips to my dentist Dr. George that I told him about Stassya and asked him if I could make an appointment for her to have a check-up. He offered to do it gratis. George had been a close neighbor of ours for many years as well as our family dentist, so we were also friends. I brought Stassya with me on my next visit. He ummmed, and nodded, poked, and prodded. I think he was very interested in the Russian dentistry methods, but finally he straightened up and looked at Stassya.

"I think I could take care of your immediate needs for approximately $3,000", he said.

"Well, we will have to wait a bit for that, I'm sure," I said.

"Thank you, Dr. George," Stassya said very politely as we walked out of his examination room. The next part of that story is a whole new chapter (which comes later).

28. Our Birthdays

"I'm old and finished," Stassya lamented one day over our morning cup of tea.

"What is it you are *complaining* about?" I asked, as I took a leisurely sip of tea, and a bite of my buttered toast.

"Forty is old in Russia," she said with regret in her voice. "I would be considered a *babushka*, [an old woman or grandmother] close to retiring, and finished with my usefulness. Anyway, my hair is turning white, and I'm getting fat," Stassya said as she ran her hands down the side of her body.

I looked at her and shook my head.

"Let's get to work, we have lots to do today," I said trying to take her mind off her silly notion.

"Life just *begins* at forty," I shot back at her as we climbed the stairs to my office.

A notion was taking place in my mind. Stassya's fortieth birthday was approaching. *She's feeling down about it so what could I do to cheer her up?* I wondered. An idea began to unfold, so I later outlined what I had in mind, and asked Jim's advice.

"That's perfect," he said immediately. "And how about adding this to your list, and you could do that, too," were his helpful suggestions.

I got to work on it on the quiet. I wanted the whole day to be a surprise. Soon the twentieth of April arrived on a beautiful spring day. Stassya and I drove Helen to school and, instead of our morning walk and cup of tea, I told Stassya to go and put on something nice—we were going out for the day. While she was dressing, I set out her tiny little chocolate cake which I had bought from Michelle Marie's bakery. I put one candle on the top, and put out a small basket with several cards sticking up.

Stassya came out of her room in her nice orange jumpsuit to my off-key singing of "Happy Birthday." She blew out her candle, and opened her funny birthday card. We laughed together, as I cut the cake in half, served our tea, and ate that little cake to the last crumb, smacking our lips.

"Now," I said, "you can open Card No. 1. But, you can't open No. 2 until I tell you."

Card No. 1: Happy Day! You have an appointment to have your nails done at my nail salon.

"Thank you, thank you, my dearest friend," was her happy response.

"Let's go then," I said. "You don't want to be late." I grabbed the basket of cards as we walked out to the car.

I was happy to see that Stassya looked as though she was savoring every moment of being pampered, her hands massaged, her nails prepared, and then she asked me to help her pick out the right color. When it was over, everyone in the shop admired Stassya's perfect nails.

As we got back into the car, I told her she could now open Card No. 2.

Card No. 2: Happy Day! Now we are going to Macy's at the mall for a complete makeup session.

"Thank you, thank you, dahling," she said, as she primped up her hair.

It wasn't difficult to find two nice young sales ladies in Macy's department store at the mall to give us a complete demonstration of their cosmetic line. We checked the mirror when they finished, and then turned to admire each other. We were delighted with our new looks, and I told Stassya to pick out a lipstick she would like.

As we passed a large display of hats against the wall of the store, we were drawn to them, as if they were magnets. Stassya is the perfect hat model, and drew the attention of both the employees and shoppers as she tried on one hat after another, posing as if for a magazine shoot. We clapped, and all enjoyed the show.

I had brought Card No. 3 into the mall with me, so I suggested we sit for a moment in the center of the mall, and I handed Stassya her next surprise.

Card No. 3: Happy Day! Lunchtime! At La Vera's.

"I'm hungry, Gayleochka! This is such a fun day, thank you."

We walked out of the mall and down Fourth Street to our favorite lunch spot, La Vera's Pizza parlor. We ordered a small pizza to share and salads. I asked the waitress if she would take our picture outside.

Stassya's Salad

Gayle and Stassya

Stassya then opened the next card.

Card No. 4: Happy Day! We are going to the movies to see Far *and* Away *with Tom Cruise and Nicole Kidman, and it includes popcorn and a drink.*

"I can't believe this day! How did you think of it? Thank you, special friend."

159

We had a little time before the afternoon movie was to start, so we wandered down Fourth Street looking in windows, laughing and talking. We ended up at the box office where I bought our tickets. We entered the theater to the intoxicating smell of hot buttered popcorn. I noticed the sign on the counter that said if you bought the large size popcorn, you could get free refills. Of course, I bought the large size, and was it large! It was a **bucket** of popcorn which we double-buttered! With that and two large cokes, we went to find our seats. Much to our surprise, even after two hours, we could not finish that bucket of popcorn, and thus did not get our free refills....

Card No. 5: Happy Day! Back to La Vera's for Gelato.

We both declined Card No. 5 and headed home, stuffed with pizza and popcorn, and feeling a little yucky. We did not have much of a party that night with Jim and Helen, but they enjoyed hearing about our eventful day, and admired Stassya's painted nails, and our beautiful makeup.

Happy Birthday!

Helen's eleventh birthday was our next major event. We planned a day at Angel Island in San Francisco Bay on May 10th. Joelle joined us. Helen was excited as she helped us put together a picnic lunch of ham and turkey sandwiches, pickles, chips, watermelon, and homemade chocolate chip cookies. We each chose a bottled drink, packed two backpacks, and drove to the little town of Tiburon to get the Angel Island ferry. It was a beautiful day, warm and sunny. San Francisco could be seen off in the distance, and we even had a peek of the Golden Gate Bridge before docking.

160

Gayle, Jim, Helen, Stassya

We started off on our hike around Angel Island and soon came to the old World War II gun emplacements. We stooped and went into the dark tunnels where the ammunition had been stored, and climbed up on the concrete slabs where the big guns had been placed to protect San Francisco Bay from enemy ships. After that, we continued on to the benches set up along the top of the cliff with great views overlooking the city of San Francisco. We could also see Alcatraz, the Bay Bridge, and the city of Oakland. There were dozens of sailboats dancing along the water and windsurfers darting here and there, and the large Golden Gate ferry boat scooted past us on its way to the ferry building at the end of Market Street in San Francisco.

Joelle and Helen

We soon made our way to another spot on the top of the island where we found picnic tables. We chose one in the sun, and basked in the warmth as we ate our lunch. We then continued our hike to the other side of the island and went into the old barracks set up as a museum depicting the life of the immigrants who came to the West Coast and were held there until they were cleared for entering the United States. Most of the immigrants had been Chinese. There were pictures to see, and stories to read, and even names scrawled on the concrete walls next to the bunk beds. It was heart-wrenching to see what some of the immigrants went through. Our spirits picked up, however, when we left that haunted place, and finished our hike back at the ferry dock, and it had been a long hike, all day, so we were weary. We sat on the lawn in the shade of the large eucalyptus trees and waited for the next ferry back to Tiburon.

"Thank you, Auntie Gayle, and Uncle Jim, and Joelle. I loved my birthday," was Helen's sweet response when we arrived home.

Happy Birthday!

My Fourth of July birthday was next. Since it could be quite hot here at home on that day, we planned a day on the shore. It was perfect with just a wisp of fog off the coast. We stopped at the Bodega Dunes campgrounds, parked the car, and walked out to the beach where we spent time picking up shells, sifting through the seaweed, and dipping our toes into the cold water. As we drove on our way along the coast, we stopped at the Salt Water Taffy shop. Helen helped me pick out a large bag of assorted salt water taffy: blueberry, strawberry/banana, maple, chocolate cream pie, coconut macaroon, mango/passionfruit, and grape. We each chose one taffy for a quick tasty treat and headed off to find lunch. We decided to stop at Lucas Wharf in Bodega Bay.

"A table by the window, please," Jim requested. "It is my wife's birthday today!" He announced to the waitress. We ordered their secret recipe—Clam Chowder. I begged for the secret ingredient as I had never found another chowder to equal that one, even in San Francisco. The waitress leaned over and whispered to me,

"It's the nutmeg, I think," she confided. So now it is out. We ate our large bowls of chowder, gorged on the delicious fresh-baked bread, and enjoyed the lovely view from the window. We munched on taffy all the way back to Santa Rosa, in time for the fireworks show at the County Fairgrounds. We arrived early enough for the music concert, spread our blankets on the lawn, and waited for the night sky. As the sky darkened, I instructed everyone to lie down.

"Heads to the center, like a spoked wheel," I ordered as we squirmed around, and laughingly bumped into each other.

"Okay, this is good, we are ready." We were lying in a circle, heads in the middle, feet to the outside, staring straight up into the sky as the "Star Spangled Banner" began to play over the loud speakers. It was magical. Oohs and aahs came from all around us with the blues, reds, greens, and bright whites flashing and booming over our heads, and appearing to drop right on top of us. It seemed to last forever, and then it was all over much too soon. We gathered up our blankets and drove home, where my perfect day ended with birthday cake and ice cream, and of course, salt water taffy.

29. Doubts and Second Thoughts

"I'm going back," Stassya blurted out one day.

"What did you say?" I asked without thinking, as I was busy with some paperwork. Then it hit me, "Wait. Wait just a minute," I said as I put my hand up. "Hold on, tell me what's wrong."

"Well, I'm living in your home, eating your food, and cleaning people's toilets for money. I'm a burden," Stassya said with tears running down her face. "I feel hopeless, my life is going nowhere. I can't do this anymore, it's not fair to you and Jim. I'm going back to Paul," she said with such sadness.

"You are doing no such thing," I said. "You wait right here; don't move!" I called over my shoulder to her as I ran upstairs to Jim.

"Stassya's threatening to go back to Russia," I told Jim as I entered the bedroom, panting, not only from running upstairs, but with my heart in my throat. "She can't go back to Paul, she's divorced and from what her mother wrote, he has another woman living with him!"

"Hold on," Jim said. "Tell me what brought this on."

"She's worried that she is a burden to us and can't see a way out of it," I said.

"She sounds like she is very lonely," Jim went on as he put the newspaper down. "She has only us, Helen, Jane, and a couple of customers who apparently like and enjoy her. She doesn't even make enough money to feed her and Helen on her own, not to mention getting her own place."

"Well, she can't go back," I retorted. "We'll have to think of something. I have an idea, at least to get her mind off it until we

164

come up with a plan."

"Now, what do you have in mind?"

"How about if I ask Joelle and Mike to babysit with Helen tonight, and we take Stassya to our dance—she likes to dance."

"And who do you have in mind to dance with her?"

"Well, you can certainly waltz, and I've seen her keeping time to the music we play—besides John teaches a lesson before the dance. You can try it out with her," I offered. "At least, she can watch and tap her foot to the music."

"You know I only feel comfortable dancing with you—I panic when I have to lead another woman and forget everything I've learned—which is not very much."

"Well, just this once won't hurt you," I countered as I dialed Joelle's number. In a few moments, it was all set up. Now the task was to descend those same stairs and inform Stassya that she was going dancing that night.

"Stassya, we've decided you are going dancing with us tonight," I announced as I entered the room.

"Dancing? How can I do that? I can't leave Helen by herself. Besides, I have nothing to wear," Stassya said. But I could see that she had perked up a bit.

"Done," I said. "Joelle and Mike are coming over. They will teach Helen a card game, and they will have lots of fun, I'm sure. And don't worry about something to wear," I added. "I have a skirt in mind and you have a nice blouse that will go with it. Jim has made an offer to dance a waltz or two with you."

"Okay, I'll come and watch you two dance," was her response. But I didn't care. I knew that once I got her there, she would participate. There would be lots of people, several singles, some just learning, and lots of great music. She would never be able to sit still.

Joelle and Mike arrived and with much laughter and fanfare, we waved goodbye, not knowing that life as we knew it that night would drastically change.

Jim parked the car, and we entered the Sebastopol Community Center. It had a stage at one end and a very large wood floor, perfect for dancing. John, the dance instructor, announced that it was time for the lesson. There were lots of eager dancers, some were already good, but many of us were beginners. We lined up in long rows, the guys facing the stage, and the gals facing the guys, one on one. Some of the women were dressed in fancy, sequined outfits, some not. Some of the men were dressed in slacks and sport shirts, and some were wearing cowboy hats and boots as if they had just come off the ranch. This was, after all, Sonoma County. The countryside was apple orchards, vineyards and grazing land. It didn't matter what you wore, everyone was eager for the lesson to begin.

Jim was in luck, the dance lesson was the rhumba, a slow dance, and he had learned it first on the cruise ship, and also had had a few lessons at John's dance studio. This was a review for him, as John taught a very basic beginning lesson before launching into a fancy turn at the end for the more advanced dancers. As we proceeded with the lesson, John had all the ladies move down one partner along the line every few minutes, to give everyone a chance to practice with partners at different levels of skill. Stassya had joined us in the lesson entering the line with the rest of the ladies. I could tell she was enjoying herself as she was animated and laughing with each new partner.

After an hour, the lesson was over, the lights were dimmed, and the music came on for an evening of dancing to various types of music. The first piece of music was rhumba, of course. Jim and I danced. Then a waltz began to play. Jim asked Stassya to be his partner, and soon they were doing the basic step all around the room. The next dance was a rhumba again. Stassya sat down as Jim asked me to dance it with him.

No sooner had Stassya sat down, when a nice-looking man came from across the room to ask her to dance. That's how life works sometimes, and this time it was Stassya's turn. As it turned out, they danced all evening together, and when they did sit down, they were chatting and laughing all the time. I watched them out of the corner of my eye. I was not surprised when Steve came up to us to introduce himself as we were getting ready to leave the dance. He asked our permission to call on Stassya some time. We smiled and said yes, of course, and teased Stassya all the way home.

Two days later, Steve called and asked Stassya out on a date, we never heard another word about "going back to Russia!"

The next Saturday night, Jim and I stayed home with Helen while Stassya went out for her first American Date Night. I could see that she was nervous and excited at the same time. There was a knock on our door. Stassya almost fell in a faint, so Jim opened the door and invited Steve inside. We chatted for a moment, Stassya introduced Helen to Steve and bent to kiss Helen goodbye. All too soon, Stassya was gone, off in the dark with a stranger.

"I feel like I just sent our daughter off on her very first date," I lamented.

I was about to go on when I remembered Helen standing there.

"Come, Sweetie," I said and took her hand. "We are going to bake cookies for your Mom." Helen happily walked into the kitchen and donned an apron. Jim put on some lively music, and we all danced around the kitchen before getting to work on our favorite chocolate chip cookies.

In our bedroom, Jim and I waited up for Stassya. I found myself glancing at the clock more than once before I heard Steve's pickup truck coming up our steep uphill driveway. In a few moments, Stassya was inside the house. Jim and I crept down the stairs hoping all went well. Stassya was smiling and humming to herself.

"You had a nice time, I see," I said with relief. I set out a plate of cookies and put on the kettle for our tea. Jim joined us, being as curious as I was.

"So?" I said. "We want to hear all about him; did you like him, will you go out again?"

"Yes and probably," she teased us with few words.

"Okay, then," I said, "I give up. Take your time and start *from the beginning.*"

"Well, we went out to dinner at a nice restaurant and talked for a couple of hours over our wine," she said.

"Okay, and then what?" I prodded.

"Then we went to a movie, and afterwards we went out for ice cream where we talked for another hour."

"Do we get any details or are you going to torture us?"

"He's very nice. I like him and we laughed a lot," Stassya finally said. "He's single and has never been married," she continued. "He lives in Rohnert Park in an apartment, and he works in construction, and he's been taking dance lessons."

That's about all we got out of her, so we said goodnight and went to bed satisfied that it seemed like she had had a very good time, and it was now well after 1 a.m.

30. Wedding Plans

Soon, Stassya and Steve became a couple. They sometimes went on Saturday or Sunday outings that included Helen, and Helen and Steve got along very well together. A few months later, Steve proposed marriage, and Stassya accepted. Amazingly, we now had a wedding to plan!

The Happy Couple

During this time, Steve encouraged Stassya to start taking driving lessons. Steve helped her practice in a large parking lot that was empty on weekends—the same one we had used with our teens when they were learning to drive. I was a little leery after our Disneyland ride where Stassya had bumped and jerked all over the Autopia track, but she did learn and soon even managed our hill.

(Several years later, Steve told us of his part in the many twists and turns that Stassya's life took:

"I had only taken a few dance lessons," Steve told us one night over dinner. "So I was very nervous about going to my first real dance. I had started off in my truck that night, got cold feet, and turned around to go back home. Then I said to myself 'What the heck,' turned around again, and went to the dance anyway. And then while I was there, much to my surprise, I saw a beautiful redhead across the room, and fell in love."

"Show them what you carry in your wallet," Stassya interrupted. Steve pulled out his wallet and showed us the tattered piece of paper with our telephone number on it!

"This always reminds me of that special evening and the amazing paths we each took to our fated meeting." Steve said with a chuckle.

"And, you captured her heart as well," I said.)

Jim and I liked Steve right from the very first time we met him. Later on, the four of us joined a session of dance classes at the John and Emily Ross Dance Studio upstairs from the Charles Schulz ice arena in Santa Rosa, California. It was to be an eight-week session of a popular dance in Sonoma County known as the Nightclub Two-Step. It has lots of twirls and turns and is very romantic. At the end of the eight-week session, the class members danced together at a performance to the song "Lady in Red". It still remains Jim's and my favorite music request at the dances we attend on our cruise ship vacations.

On one of our earlier cruises, Jim and I had enjoyed the music of one small band for dancing in one of the lounges. It was a husband and wife team called the Walking Miracles. They both sang and played instruments. This was a cruise to Hawaii, and we had the opportunity to get to know them personally one day when we met them outside on deck during a day at sea. After three or four days into the cruise, they would begin to play "Lady in Red" every time we entered the lounge. (To our delight, six years later, the Walking Miracles were playing in the lounge on our Australian cruise, and played "Lady in Red" again as we entered the lounge. We had recognized each other immediately!)

Meanwhile, the wedding plans were beginning to take shape. Things had settled down a little in Russia so Stassya's mother Sophia was able to obtain a visitor's visa in time to come for the bridal shower, wedding ceremony, and reception. Sophia brought a bag of dried Russian mushrooms from the Russian forest. She cooked us a delicious Russian mushroom soup. It was not anything like American cream of mushroom soup. It had a clear broth and was excellent. No wonder Stassya was excited when she saw all those mushrooms right near our home, and thank goodness I was with her when she had started to pick them for our dinner that night. I had panicked because with those particular mushrooms, it could have easily been our last meal!

Sophia (Helen's grandmother), Helen, and Stassya

While the wedding ceremony was still in the planning stage, Stassya asked Jim to give her away, I was to be her matron of honor, and Helen, the flower girl. Nancy, Helen's friend Debbie's mother, suggested using her family's church for the ceremony.

Me, the wedding couple, and Steve's best man

Leaving the church for the reception

It was a happy day, full of love and laughter. After the reception at the local community center, Stassya and Steve left on their honeymoon to Hawaii; Helen went home to their new apartment with her grandmother. Jim and I went home to an empty house.

31. Mrs. Stassya Pacheco

One of our favorite shopping outings was to take the free bus which, back in the early 1990s, was provided by Nordstrom Department Store in Corte Madera, about a forty-five minute drive south of Santa Rosa. The bus would pick up eager shoppers at the Veteran's Building parking lot near our home. Not only was the bus free but Nordstrom also provided a special VIP lounge at our disposal with snacks and drinks. We took this local trip several times, and happily spent the day in Nordstrom and the other shops in that outdoor mall. Sadly, this offer was eventually canceled when a Nordstrom department store moved into the Santa Rosa Mall.

Sometime after Stassya's wedding, and after she had moved from our home, I drove over to her and Steve's new apartment to pick her up for one of our bus trips to Nordstrom. I rang the doorbell, and was met by a panicked, red-faced woman standing in a large puddle of soap suds. It was an amazing sight!

"Hurry, hurry," Stassya said as she pulled me into the entry which was right off the kitchen. "I think I used too much soap in the dishwasher!"

"You sure did, and the wrong kind," I said as I spied the concentrated dishwashing liquid soap bottle standing on the counter. "You are supposed to use dishwasher *detergent* in a dishwasher not *concentrated liquid soap*. Grab a large bowl," I said. I took off my shoes and waded into the kitchen through the mound of soap suds still spilling out of the dishwasher. We each grabbed a bowl and started to scoop the bubbles into the sink. We finally cleared enough away so that we could open the dishwasher and clean it out. Then we mopped up the kitchen and entry floors. After that, we had a good

172

laugh, a cup of tea, and missed our shopping trip that day.

During one of her visits to Steve's sister's home in Sacramento, Stassya had asked her about her job as a dental assistant. After hearing about her sister-in-law's job, Stassya told her about all the dental work she needed to have done, and how much it would cost her. Steve's sister told Stassya that she could get a degree at her local junior college, and become an assistant herself, and would then perhaps be able to get her dental work done for nothing or at least a discount. That sounded like a good idea to Stassya, so she immediately enrolled at Santa Rosa Junior College. She graduated two years later with high honors, and began her new career. But, for her, it was not enough that she have the degree, so she studied for an additional certificate that allowed her to do some additional procedures that required more training. At the time, only 600 assistants in California had qualified for the RDA (Registered Dental Assistant) certificate.

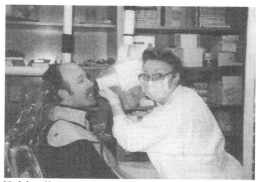

Pointing to her lapel pin.   *Hold still, Honey!*

Now Stassya finally had her own car, and she and Steve were soon to have their own home. Jane, our Russian friend's husband was an architect. Steve and Stassya hired him to design their home and supervise its construction after they had found a nice, large lot in Santa Rosa and purchased it. Soon a beautiful two-story home was going up. After they moved in, Stassya came dashing into my home one day, all excited.

"You won't believe this," she said as she took off her shoes at the door and slipped her feet into her waiting slippers. "I met my new neighbor this morning. You'll never guess who it is!"

"Well, you might just tell me and save me all those guesses," I said.

"Remember that belly dancer Marilyn invited to one of our classes when I came here with my students?"

"Barely," I laughed.

"She's my next-door neighbor, Sally! She came over to introduce herself, and we both recognized each other."

"She was all dressed in costume that day. How did you know who it was?"

"When she realized that I am Russian, she asked me if I was the teacher of the Russian class she had danced for."

"What a coincidence!" I just shook my head. *Life with you has been one coincidence after another,* I thought to myself. *What is next?*

Before Steve and Stassya furnished their home, Steve bought Stassya a grand piano. Stassya loved classical music and was also a talented pianist. They placed it in the living room in front of the picture window, and Jim and I were excited when they invited us for Stassya's first personal concert in her home. It wasn't long before she found a group of women who enjoyed playing duets, and then they branched into two-piano foursomes and played together whenever possible. Jim and I attended several of their concerts usually in one of their homes, and occasionally at a community center. All of the women were very talented, some taught private piano lessons. Stassya had also taught piano over the past years both in Russia and here in the United States.

Steve grew up on a farm, so he was eager to plant fruit trees on their new property. Over the years as the plants grew, Stassya supplied us with lemons, peaches, nectarines, and other edibles they grew in their garden. Steve also constructed a koi pond complete with a fountain. The koi were big and very colorful. Each one even had their own name. The largest yellow one was named "Pineapple".

Prior to meeting Steve, Stassya had applied for American citizenship. After she was married, she considered reapplying as the wife of an American, but found out that it would take longer than the application she had already filed, since she would have to start over again. As it was, the process at that time of becoming an American citizen with an American passport took over ten years.

Stassya's application was accepted and a date set for her citizenship ceremony in San Francisco. Unfortunately Helen had passed the age to be included as Stassya's underage daughter, so Helen had to begin her own application. By the time she applied, it no longer took ten years.

Jim and I went with Stassya to the citizenship swearing-in ceremony in San Francisco. We were surprised to see such a large auditorium filled with new Americans! The atmosphere was charged with such excitement and emotion that I had tears running down my face. To see all these new Americans so grateful to become one of us was a very moving experience I will never forget. Being part of that really made me appreciate my grandmother's experience. (My grandmother arrived in New York at age seventeen, having left her parents behind in Sweden, to begin a new life. What courage that must have taken in the late 1800s. Just this year, I had the privilege of standing on the dock in Goteborg, Sweden, where my grandmother boarded her boat for the shores of America. I wondered if she was scared, sad, excited, or happy; maybe all of that. While I stood on that dock that day, I looked out to sea and whispered, *Thank you, Grandma.)*

Stassya was sitting in the auditorium with the large group of new citizens. Jim and I were sitting in the balcony. I could see Stassya because she was wearing our matching dress. A color-guard marched in carrying the flag. Everyone was asked to stand to sing the "Star-Spangled Banner". The new citizens remained standing for the Oath of Allegiance read from the stage by an officer of the U.S. Citizen and Immigration Services. With all right hands raised high, each new American pledged their oath. As they left the auditorium, they were given their certificates. Cameras were snapping, people were smiling from ear to ear, handshakes and hugs were happening everywhere; congratulations could be heard above the noise. Stassya was so excited when she ran up to us, she nearly knocked us over!

Happy New American and sponsor

"Thank you, thank you, my dahlings," she said as she waved her miniature American flag. We grabbed each other around the waist and skipped out of the auditorium with Jim following closely behind. We found a small coffee and ice cream shop around the corner.

"Ladies," Jim called out, "let's duck in here and have a little snack to celebrate, and then head out of the city before the commuters start their daily fight for space." Jim held the door for us as he continued, "I am no match for those experienced freeway commuter-time drivers!"

As we entered the coffee shop, there was music playing. Stassya grabbed Jim and began to dance around the little floor. It looked like a combination of a Russian jig and a waltz, but Stassya was so happy, it didn't matter.

Celebratory dance at the coffee shop

Before Helen received her citizenship, Stassya and Steve made the decision to send her to Russia to visit her grandmother and her father. By that time, she was seventeen years old and eligible to visit with a special visitor's visa. Helen enjoyed her visit with her grandmother, and renewed her family ties with her Aunt Nina and her two boy cousins. Helen also visited her father, and met his new wife and her daughter who was about eight years old. Even though Helen had enjoyed her visit, she was very grateful to be back home in the United States with her mom and Steve. Upon her return, Helen asked Steve to formally adopt her. To her, he was now her father. When Helen was in her high school English class, she told us that her teacher was amazed when she found out that English was not Helen's first language. However, Stassya told us that Helen's Russian language remained elementary. Helen went on to continue her education in college and become a registered nurse. (I still receive birthday and holiday cards from Helen, always thanking us for bringing her to America.)

During their first years together, Steve had a dream of moving to the state of Washington near Puget Sound where he could have a boat to use for fishing. Steve and Stassya made several trips to Washington, and finally settled on Mount Vernon. Mount Vernon is about half way between Seattle and Vancouver and is in a "banana belt" area. Protected by islands situated off the coast, they have very pleasant weather and don't get the cold winds and abundant rain Washington State is known for. In April and May, the whole area abounds in fields of beautiful, colorful tulips as far as the eye can see.

They bought a brand-new home up on a bluff, backed up to a beautiful forest. In January of 2012, we visited them on our way to Lake Louise, Canada, for the International Ice Carving Festival. We arrived just as did the worst snow storm to ever hit the Seattle and Mount Vernon areas. We stayed for three days. Since I had asked Stassya to order snow for me, I have been blamed for shutting down the whole state including shopping malls and schools!

We enjoyed walking through the quiet, snow-covered forest behind Stassya and Steve's home. We watched from a window as a mother deer and her two babies came into their backyard to feed.

One of the babies was very unusual as its color was white. While deer are common around their yard, Stassya had never seen that little one before. We took lots of pictures before the doe gathered her little ones and disappeared into the forest. (Stassya has told me she has never seen them since.)

The babe in white

Stassya and me walking in the snowy forest

The following December, we went again to Mt. Vernon and invited Stassya to join us on the snow train excursion to Leavenworth, a small Swiss-like village in the Cascade Mountains outside of Seattle. We enjoyed the train ride with the beautiful scenery outside, the fun activities onboard, and the delicious box lunch served at our seat. We had entertainment all day coming through our train car, from a family singing group to two magicians playing amazing card tricks. My favorite was a trio of musicians, one of them a woman who was playing a raucous Russian dance on her accordion. I leaned over to Stassya,

"Go on, get up and do your Russian dance," I said to her.

"No, no," Stassya said dipping her head down.

I gave her a little push, and said, "Go on, everyone would love it!"

Stassya finally gave in, got up, and began her Russian dance in the aisle of the train accompanied by hoots and hollers and lots of clapping. Everyone did love it, and I think Stassya did, too. When it was over, I saw that mischievous smile as she sat down next to me.

Stassya's Russian dance on the Leavenworth Snow Train

Leavenworth was a beautiful little village all decked out for Christmas. It looked as if we had stepped into a real Swiss alpine village covered in snow. There were lots of boutique shops with ornaments and gifts from all over Europe. There were bonfires in the snow-covered street where we could warm our hands and lots of places to eat. And when it got dark, all the decorative lights came on in a special ceremony. Every shop was decorated with little twinkling lights, and the large evergreen tree in the square was lit from top to bottom and on every branch. All the visitors that day, hundreds of them, were crowded into the streets and into the square to hear the Christmas music being played over the loudspeakers. It was a beautiful sight, but all too soon it was over for us, as we had to get back to the train station for our ride back down the mountain.

After spending some days at Stassya's home visiting with her and Helen, (Steve was working at the time in Alaska) it was time for Jim and I to say goodbye once again and head home. As Stassya dropped us off at the train station in Mount Vernon, she pointed out the large colorful poster hanging on the wall. It showed a picture of the latest simulcast opera to be shown at the small vintage theater located in downtown Mount Vernon. We had visited the theater with Stassya the day before. She had given us a tour. It had red velvet seats, colorful red wall coverings, and antique lights hanging from the high ceiling. The poster at the station had a list of the season's operas. Down in the corner, there was a picture of Stassya and a description of her role in giving a pre-performance lecture describing the storyline and history of each opera before its showing. I asked her once if she read from her notes.

"No, dahling," she said as she shook her head. "I just tell the story as I would tell it to you at your dining room table."

I know that with her charming accent she would hold the audience spellbound just as I had been when listening to this expert story teller, during the years of our friendship.

Then came another tearful good-bye, as we boarded the train with promises to visit each other soon.

32. Twenty-five Years Later

This year, 2014, is Stassya's twenty-fifth anniversary of her very first visit to our home in Santa Rosa in December of 1989. She came to visit us from her home in Washington State as part of our celebration, and slept in the same room Jim and I had decorated so lovingly all those years ago when she and Helen first came and lived with us for almost two years. We had recently turned it back into a bedroom after having used it as my business office for the previous fifteen years.

Stassya brought her cleaned and pressed matching dress. We tried them on. The dresses were a bit snug, but we posed for another picture, looking a bit older and perhaps wiser, still best friends, but again, worlds' apart (though this time, states' apart).

When I look back to the image of Stassya sitting on our white sofa with her red, henna-colored hair, her proud bearing, and wearing her bright pink sweater with wide stripes, I can't help but think of my opening remark, *What is happening in Russia?* What if, instead, I had said, *Stanislava, you are going to be my best friend. You are going to become an American citizen, marry a very nice American man, learn to drive a car and own one, actually two of them, live in a house with a fruit orchard and a koi pond with a fountain, own a boat, go on a couple of cruises, one of them to Tahiti.*

What if I had said, *Stanislava, you are going to steal my heart, and the heart of many people with whom you will come in contact. You are going to blossom after the age of forty, not wither and be considered the babushka you thought you might become.* What if I had told you, *Stanislava, that your life was only just beginning!* It would have sounded like complete nonsense at the time.

With her natural charm, knowledge, and enthusiasm, Stassya makes a mark wherever she goes. She stands out in a crowd, as she did when the actress Lindsay Wagner spied her and wanted to join our group in Leningrad during our palace tour; when she brought an excited group together at her daughter's school in Santa Rosa, offering to cook a Russian dinner and talk about all things Russian; when she inspired a student body, introducing them to her favorite classical music; and as she did when she stood out in the crowd, winning Steve's heart across the dance floor—the same evening she was about to give up and return to Russia, just hours earlier.

She is a loving and caring friend to those who gather close to her, and especially, most of all to me. She captured my heart and my mind a long time ago, inspiring me to expand my interests to ballet, opera, and symphony music concerts. We have laughed, cried, and shared our thoughts, hopes and dreams. Living in small, close quarters with Stassya and Helen for nearly two years made Jim and I more tolerant, understanding, and able to compromise with each other in our own everyday lives. It was so rewarding for us to watch both Stassya and Helen, as they became more and more confident in their new lives, each realizing her own potential.

We declared early on in our friendship that we would spend our last years sitting in our rocking chairs and writing our story. Since I am twelve years older than Stassya, I could not wait any longer to put down on paper what has been in my heart all these years.

We have traced the lineage of our chance meeting from one small moment in Russia thousands of miles to another small moment in California. How could something that would become so important to the two of us just happen? We changed each other's lives completely. Why did Stassya's dream of becoming a concert pianist have to be put aside? Why did she have to give up teaching German for English—a language she did not know? What led her to apply for the job at School #160 just at the moment when they had an opening? Why did Tom Areton of Cultural Homestay International choose School #160 to visit and offer them his plan of a school exchange? Why did his wife Lilka suggest that we host Stanislava in our home?

On the other hand, what pushed me to read the want ads in my very small local newspaper on the very day an ad showed up asking for applicants for a job with CHI? When asked by the interviewer

Marilyn what my goals were, I told her I wanted her job as Area Administrator. That never happened, as I was asked to develop a new department called the "Outbound Office". This put me in a position to send American students abroad to study, and to accept and mentor long-term foreign students in my area. When the Russian program became available, Marilyn and I were asked to lead the first incoming group, and I was asked to take the first group to Russia.

Why was Russia available for just such a program at just this moment in time? How easily Stassya and I could have missed one another at each step of the way. And, the last step: How did Stassya and Helen slip out of Russia at just the right moment in time—it was such a close call....

Where have those years gone?

EPILOGUE

Helen Pavlovna Nazarova, Today

(written by Helen at my request in November 2015; unedited)

I don't remember what pre-conceived notions I had about life in America. The trip happened so suddenly I had very little time to actually plan and think. I was able to put together ideas in my mind's eye from the pictures and photographs, as well as stories told by mom, American movies, and just plain imagination. Overall, I came to imagine America to be a happy and wonderful place, where everybody else wanted to go, and only the lucky chosen few had the opportunity. I thought of it as a place of smiling and happy people who drove luxurious cars, wore beautiful clothes, drank Coca-Cola, and ate potato chips from fancy packages.

Before coming to this new land, I knew that I would have to work hard and learn the language, attend a new school, be on my best behavior, and not disappoint my mother or our American friends. And since everything happened so fast, it felt like a "dive into unknown waters" head first. Staying in this country permanently was not ever a thought or a possibility in my mind. I remember fantasizing about how "cool" I would be to my peers after my return back to Russia in three months. As the girl who went to America, I would have so many stories and experiences to share with my friends. They would have no choice but to be green with envy. Secretly I imagined myself having something of a celebrity status upon my return!

I have to say that as usual, my mom was the true hero. She did not sleep for seventy-two hours as she frantically prepped for our departure. She was able to secure passports and proper documentation, to purchase flight tickets with the money provided by Jim and Gayle, arrange for transportation to the airport, and break the news to my father who was unwilling to help or provide any support. All this had to happen in a climate of political uncertainty and chaos, which Russia had turned into within the last year.

Finally, with what was $20 in her pocket, we sat at the Pulkovo airport in St. Petersburg, enduring the delay of twelve hours due to unfavorable weather and flying conditions prior to finally boarding the aircraft on the way to America. This was my first experience flying and for the majority of the flight, it was night and dark outside. I recall staring out the window into nothingness, but all the same it was fascinating, kind of scary, and absolutely breathtaking. Our first stop in America was actually in New York, at Kennedy airport. We had to wait overnight for a connecting flight to California due to that long delay prior to our departure from St. Petersburg. My mom spent that last $20 on McDonalds for our dinner, which was the first time I had fast food and French fries! What a treat! She made a bed for me on top of our suitcase placed upon those uncomfortable metal chairs, and she once again stayed up all night waiting until morning and the opportunity to continue the journey.

We finally arrived in San Francisco and were met by Jim and Gayle. They drove us to their home, now also our new temporary home, in their beautiful fancy car with leather seats, and climate-control air conditioning. That was my first true taste of American luxury.

The first few weeks or so at the home of Jim and Gayle was a very happy time. First of all I have never seen such a beautiful and comfortable home! It was so clean, with white carpets and all the conveniences of modern appliances. We had a room downstairs, which had a sliding door and a patio. We could just sit and enjoy the fantastic weather and listen to the birds. I remember the delicious dinners of pork chops and sweet potatoes, and how the whole house smelled so wonderful and all of us sitting at the dining room table, talking and expressing ourselves. I remember that my mom was so happy for the time being to get away from Russia, from her husband, and from the stress of everyday life.

Gayle and Jim provided us with such a warm welcome. They opened up their home and their world to us. They treated us like family. This act of kindness and friendship has forever left a deep impression on my heart and soul. They had been our guests in Russia; they knew our stories and about our struggles. They sacrificed a lot and changed our lives, giving us this beautiful opportunity to come to America to visit. The story of this experience

186

is both very "feel good", but also powerful and motivational. They shared with us so many wonderful experiences and "firsts" of being in this new culture, providing so much support. Together we celebrated American holidays for the first time, traveled to Disneyland and Universal Studios which created such vivid and colorful memories. For a child of ten years of age, this was the most exciting and amazing time, with experiences I had never even dreamed of!

The very first holiday I experienced in America was Halloween. This was a holiday completely unknown to me, and I think it took a while to understand the concept of dressing up in costumes and going to stranger's houses asking for candy! However, I was soon very excited about this spooky holiday, and my first costume was as a black cat.

My first Christmas in their home was another memory I cherish so fondly. In Russia Christmas was not celebrated during those years of my youth. Our winter holiday was celebrating the New Year with the tree. Presents and all the festivities were for the kids. However, the American Christmas celebration was so much more grand with the holiday season lasting the whole month of December. Gayle really made this season special for me. We counted down the days to the big day by using an advent calendar, which is something she did for her daughter, Joelle.

Not everything about this new environment was easy, and I had to face some challenges. While first being enrolled in an American school, which was fifth grade at the time, I learned that not everybody is nice and friendly, especially kids of my own age. Being different looking, wearing clothes out of style, having limited language skills, and a strange accent made me a target for bullies and isolated. I did not make friends right away. This was very different from my experiences in Russia. I had lots of friends at my school in Russia. However, no matter what, I was determined to learn the language and the culture, which happened so naturally because I was immersed in this experience.

It was not difficult to learn English after I came to America. The only times I spoke in Russian was with my mom, while everybody else in my life now spoke in English. Being that young I was able to pick up on it with ease and fairly quickly. When I finally was able to converse in English, I found that in any school or social club I attended, I was the only one from Russia. This made me unique and special. It added to other people's curiosity and they wanted to ask me questions about Russia, or wanted to hear me speak Russian. Soon I was able to use this to my advantage in making conversation and socializing with my peers, and eventually making friends. Together my mom and I learned and experienced life in America, with all the adjustments and facing the unknown. I think that because of this my mom and I have a very special bond. My mom's contagious personality and genuine warmth towards people have gained her many friends and admirers.

Another time, good fortune came into our lives after we moved to America was when my mom met my step-dad Steve. She met him while we were living at Gayle and Jim's home, about a year and a half into our stay. At this point in time we were deciding on what to do with our future. While the decision had been made to remain in America and go through the immigration process, it was still a time of more questions than answers. My mom was also going through a divorce from my father in Russia and petitioning for full custody of me. This was a challenge and a battle. For many years before getting my actual citizenship, there was always this concern regarding having to be deported.

My mom met my step-dad Steve by chance on the urge of Gayle and Jim to go out with them dancing one evening. When recapping this story with my mom, she remembers how discouraged and worried she was feeling regarding our future in America and what choices we had to make. It was at this unlikely time and by total chance that she met a man and they fell in love, which eventually led to a marriage and start of a new family. After first meeting at that dance, mom and Steve quickly became an item. Steve was drawn to my mother because she was beautiful and unique from the rest of the women. She was different, as he later recalled. And she saw in him a good-natured and level-headed man. It truly seemed like they were meant for each other with fate bringing the two together. Within a few months they were engaged and soon married. While Steve did not have children of his own, his fatherly instincts were very good and he was a good role model and protective male figure in my life. We bonded as a family over road trips, going out to the coast, camping, and playing back yard sports. Soon after their marriage, I was legally adopted by Steve.

I left my homeland as a child and returned back a young woman. That was a very special trip back, because it was so important for me to reconnect with my family members. So much of the world had changed. By the time I made that first trip in 1997, it

188

seemed as if the majority of the turmoil Russia underwent after the collapse of Communism, was over. The streets were once again safer and society functioned under order. After years of uncertainty and hardship, which I recall during my last year in Russia prior to relocating to America; as if by popular demand, normalization was favored. Once again Russia triumphed over adversity.

However the simplicity of everyday living was still present out in the country. Going back to Russia, especially that first time, felt like I was stepping back in time. My beloved *dacha* remained mostly unchanged, although perhaps more dilapidated, but still dear to my heart. Same rusty train station, same pot-holed, dirt roads, same green wooden house with hand-painted white trim, same forests, same brown river water, same pleasant simplicity of yesteryear.

The dacha (commonly called the summer place) that Stassya's father built.

The summer place (*dacha*) was a happy place, filled with many childhood memories I enjoy thinking about to this day. Twenty miles out of city limits, it was a lush and green paradise away from the grit and the hustle and bustle of the city. Looking forward to staying at the summer place meant no school, spending time with my grandparents, eating fresh fruits and veggies from the garden, and staying out late past the usual bedtime. It was a safe place where kids could ride their bikes, visit with friends and swim in the river on the warmer days. All the local families had known each other for generations which gave the entire place a feeling of closeness and familiarity.

Inside our green wooden house, we had all the necessary amenities needed for a comfortable life. We had an old refrigerator (from the 30's), black and white TV, comfortable beds, running water (from the river), traditional Russian wood-burning stove to keep the whole house warm, plenty of furniture and household items. The most amazing thing is that the house was entirely built by hand by my grandfather and grandmother in the 1950s, after the war. My grandparents were avid gardeners, planting not only vegetables and berry bushes, but also beautiful flowers, which really brightened and beautified the place. The dacha was a place to bond with my grandparents, aunt, cousins, great aunts and second cousins who lived across the river. We shared fresh strawberries. We built bon fires and baked home-grown potatoes right in the coals. Our family would venture out for hours into the forests for seasonal mushrooming in the early fall/late summer. My aunt Nina was a particular enthusiast, and knew all the "secret spots". She taught me enough about mushrooming that I could decipher poison ones from the edible ones. The mushrooms were used for making soups and frying up with potatoes. Being in the forest was like being hypnotized and I would become disoriented. Luckily, the grown-ups always knew their way home, no matter how far we ventured out.

Even as a child, I understood and was fascinated with the history of the place. World War II was literally fought in the forests surrounding our *dacha*, and many war-time artifacts and skeletons of fallen soldiers have been found over the years.

While America is where I made my life what it is today, and is where I belong, I cannot deny that Russia is my homeland. I feel a definite spiritual connection to the city of St. Petersburg, and to the land. I went back again in 2003 and plan to return, perhaps next year. I know that a lot more has changed, and I will not recognize my summer place. The old green house with white trim has been replaced with a modular modern home. I wonder how I will feel when I return once again.

Helen's second visit to Russia, 2003

While the American school and educational system was not as strict as the Russian one, I took to my studies knowing that hard work and discipline would eventually pay off. My goals in life at that time were to eventually go to college and to be involved in a career which would make me independent. I chose healthcare. I started with dental hygiene and worked at that career for some time. Then I went back to college and took courses in nursing. I am a registered nurse both in California and in Washington.

Since I moved to Washington to be closer to my mother and Steve, I have been working in a nursing home, a live-in care center. I am the RN on night duty, and am the shift supervisor. I have my own apartment and enjoy spending some of my free time at the local spa/gym, taking belly dancing classes with my mother, and attending the operas and listening to my mother describe the history and story lines of the various simulcast operas offered at our local theater.

It is such an honor to me that you, (Gayle) are writing the memoir of our stories of friendship and the journey from Russia to America! It is so wonderful and remarkable how our paths have crossed years ago. The story which had resulted is both touching and

191

exciting! I vividly remember first experiencing being in America and the newness and the excitement that I felt. I felt like the luckiest and most blessed person! Some of my fondest memories are the Christmases and holiday celebrations, trips to Disneyland and the family get-togethers, and such sweet warm days. From the bottom of my heart and soul thank you again for taking such good care of me and my mom, and for helping our future.

Stanislava Vladislavouna Nazarova Pacheco (Stassya)

Even though Stassya accepted housecleaning jobs like many other new immigrants, she is highly educated, talented, and was always determined to succeed. She has three college degrees, one in music, one in teaching, and now also one as a dental assistant.

Stassya had been accepted into the college of music in Leningrad at age fifteen. For four years, she attended classes for more than forty hours a week, six days a week, studying history, religion, piano, voice training, choir, harmony, conducting, orchestration, and composition. She also learned to play all the instruments of the Russian folk orchestra and to compose music for each instrument.

Stassya, from an early age had aspired to be a concert pianist. I was amazed at her skill, not only with classical music, but with *all* kinds, from Russian folksongs to American tunes. The early stages of arthritis in her hands, however, took that dream away from her. In looking for another way to earn her living in Russia, she decided to go back to college and study to be a teacher. Since she had studied German in school and was proficient in it, she went to the Pedagogical Institute in Leningrad to apply for a degree to teach German. But however by the time Stassya applied for the German course, it was full. She had the choice of several other subjects, so she chose English.

"I thought it would be fun to learn what the Beatles were singing, so I applied for the English course," she told me.

"And?" I asked.

"I had to laugh when I discovered they were repeating the same words over and over again, but by that time, I was aware that I had an aptitude for languages, and was enjoying learning English," she said. "After I graduated, I got a job at School #160, one of the few schools in Leningrad immersing students in English."

Stassya told me that compared to the reign of Stalin, living and growing up during the Communist regime of the 1950s and 1960s under Khrushchev, was a good and prosperous time in Leningrad. In the large cities food was plentiful, though not necessarily much of a variety, and some foreign movies were allowed. In fact, French movies would be featured for one week, and then the popular Italian movies with Sophia Loren would be run for a week. High school groups from England would come on tours, staying in hotels and visiting the highlights. University students from the USA came to study the Russian language for six-week courses during the summer. It was during this time that Lilka Areton of Cultural Homestay International, at 19 years old, visited Russia, and drove around with a friend in a little red car.

At that time politics was a sticky subject in Communist Russia. Who you knew and bribery got you what you wanted, but for the most part, people were satisfied that they had a good life. They knew if there was a long line in front of a shop, there was something good at the end, and would wait patiently to buy whatever it was. Cooking was sometimes a challenge, and so creativity was a great asset. There were no recipes so making each meal was an adventure, which of course we discovered when Stassya took over the cooking for me in our home.

When Stassya met Steve Pacheco at a dance in Santa Rosa, little did she realize her life would take another sharp turn. After their marriage, she decided to go back to college yet again and earned her degree to become a dental assistant but even that was not enough for her, as she took the courses which qualified for the additional RDA certificate offered in California allowing her to perform additional more technical duties as the dentist's assistant.

When Steve and Stassya moved to Washington State a few years ago, they bought a brand-new home on a lot that backs up to a beautiful forested area. One of their upstairs windows looks out to a long-distance view of the majestic snow-covered peak of Mount Baker.

Stassya immediately became active in her community by offering to give thirty-minute historical talks on each of the operas shown by simulcast in their local movie theater every two weeks.

The poster advertising this event is put up all over Mount Vernon and surrounding towns. It displays Stassya's picture with a description of her half-hour talks prior to the live transmission. She has a strong following, which doesn't surprise me one bit!

Stassya has also joined a group of ladies who are not native-born Americans. They are originally from France, Switzerland, England, Germany, Russia, and other countries from around the world. They take turns meeting once a month at one of the homes bringing food to share. They also share their experiences—both sad and funny—and understand each other's struggles to assimilate into a new country, culture, language, customs, and food. Through Stassya I have been able to see how discouraging it can be to feel a part of a new world and how a support group like this can be a blessing.

The last time we visited Stassya and Steve at their home, we were very surprised at the secret they had kept from us for two months. They took us for a ride after breakfast one day and stopped at a marina. We walked among the many boats moored next to the dock when Steve pointed out a very large elegant yacht for sale for a very expensive price. He said they wanted to buy it. Of course, we laughed at his joke and continued laughing as he turned around and pointed to a smaller but very nice boat moored nearby and said, "But we bought this one instead. Come on, I'll show it to you." We snickered and went along with his "joke". As he invited us up onto the boat, we began to think it may not be a joke after all and began to question him, "Are you serious?"

"Of course," he said. "Come have some soda and chocolates!" During our tour of the boat, Stassya made a point to inform us that since it includes a toilet and shower, it is not just a boat, but a yacht.

Jim named Steve, Captain Treacherous. Stassya is his First Mate—this lady who drove the Autopia car in Disneyland in fits and jerks not so many years ago! *Give me a life jacket, please!*

Captain Treacherous and First Mate Stassya

Stassya, age 13

Stanislava Vladislavouna Nazarova Pacheco (Stassya)

Our young family, 1973 – Jim, David, age 10,
Andrew, age 11, Gayle, and Joelle, age 4

Gayle, age 21   *Jim, age 21*

Gayle Elizabeth Johnson Peebles, author

My father came to California from Duluth, Minnesota, in 1942 where he found work at the Lockheed airplane factory in Burbank producing planes for the war effort. My mother and I soon followed. I was one and a half years old, but I can still remember sitting on the train. Maybe that began my love to travel.

Or maybe it was in the fifth grade when my assignment was to choose a country for an oral report. I was unbelievably shy, but was so interested in my subject that I was not bothered by my usual desire to fade into the background. I had chosen Sweden, as my Swedish grandmother had emigrated from Sweden at age seventeen, married, and raised her family in Minnesota. She lived in California with us during winters when I was young, and had taught me a few Swedish words, and gave me a little magic trick which I used in my oral report.

Or maybe it was in the sixth grade when we studied Greece and Egypt. I was fascinated by pictures of the ruins and pyramids in my textbook.

After I graduated from high school, I chose to go to school in Minnesota for a year as I wanted to experience a snowy winter. My cousins could all ski and ice skate, and could make snowmen—I was jealous. I wanted to experience all of that and did. I think I drove my fellow students in the dorm crazy when I knocked on doors early in the mornings to find someone to go ice skating with me before school started. They paid me back when they asked me to play 'Crack the Whip' with them on the frozen-over school playground across the street. I was honored when they placed me on the end. I wobbled and held on for dear life as they turned faster and faster. I became dizzy, lost my hold, and plunged off into a soft snow drift and then, I actually asked them to do it again!

Back home in California the following winter, my high school best girlfriend Carol, and I decided to go to New York, and find work as secretaries. After we found an apartment, we tramped the streets of Manhattan in the winter snow until eventually we were both offered jobs at the new Time and Life building. Through a friend of Carol's family, we met a girl from Puerto Rico who we asked to share our apartment with us. Marta was studying at the Academy of Dramatic Arts. Her father was the president of the House of Representatives in San Juan. Marta was very much against the proposal that Puerto Rico become a state instead of remaining a possession of the United States. We had many midnight discussions on this subject. Several months later, Marta invited us to spend Memorial Day weekend at her parent's home in San Juan. That was my first official visit outside of the United States besides driving with my parents a few times to Tijuana, Mexico as a day trip.

Then after six months, Carol and I returned home, rented an apartment together in Hollywood, and both soon got secretarial jobs at Capitol Records. Jim had surprised me by meeting me at the airport when I arrived from New York. We had dated off and on for four years and began to date once again. We enjoyed going to the Hollywood Bowl to see Nat King Cole, and to the Greek Theater to see Johnny Mathis. We also went dancing at the Hollywood Palladium and to the Santa Monica Pier. We soon became engaged, and were married a few months later in 1962, and began our family of ultimately three children. Vacations in those early years were spent camping at the beach, in Yosemite, in the Redwoods, and in Canada.

During those early years our home was in San Bernardino, California. It seemed to me to be over one hundred degrees six months out of the year. I was not happy with all that heat and smog. It took a driving trip across the country to Ohio to visit Jim's relatives, and to Minnesota to visit mine before I spoke up. Everything was green and moist almost as soon as we left the deserts of California and Arizona on Route 66. When I finally gave an ultimatum to Jim, he gave up and agreed to look for another place to live, work, and raise our family. We looked at San Diego, and Santa Barbara, before we settled on Santa Rosa in Northern California.

We arrived in Santa Rosa with everything we owned on January 1, 1975. It seemed as if it rained 40 days and nights—I was in heaven. Everything was green and moist in the winter, and turned golden in the summer with the average temperature of eighty degrees in the summer afternoons, and the morning and evening fog to cool it down.

I was a stay-at-home mom until all three children were finally in school, and then got a part-time job which gave me "mommy's" hours. Then in 1982, I saw an article in the newspaper asking for host families for a group of foreign students coming for a three week visit. They were coming from Sweden, the country of my grandmother! We chose seventeen-year-old Sten, as he was about the age of our two sons. We had such a good time with him that I was hooked. The next summer, we took on a very young girl from Japan. She was the same age as our daughter Joelle, twelve years old. Although neither one of the girls spoke each other's language, they still laughed and had fun together. My daughter wrote a touching essay about that experience when she was in college.

This program was through my next-door neighbor who was the coordinator of the local homestay program. I volunteered for everything from driving to helping in the classroom. When the program was over, I asked the area representative if I could do what my neighbor was doing, and was told that they could only use one person in our town.

By chance, one day a few months later, I was browsing through our local newspaper, doing the crossword puzzle which happened to be on the page across from the listing of job opportunities. A new organization, Cultural Homestay International, was advertising for local area coordinators for Japanese groups coming for three-week homestays the following summer. I called and went for an interview. That led to my working for CHI for twenty years, and ultimately I became the English teacher for over 500 Japanese students from junior high age to adults. Then I added the job of coordinating CHI's semester and year programs for high school students coming from abroad. I found the host families for the students, and enrolled them in the local high schools in Sonoma and Napa counties.

I went on to become the assistant area coordinator. After that, I was asked to develop the new program to send American students to study abroad for both short, three-week homestays, and for high school semester and year-long programs. I began the Outbound Office in my home and gradually expanded to a nice office building near my home. During this time, I put together familiarization (fam) trips for the staff of CHI to visit our partner organizations in New Zealand, Australia, Germany, Italy, and Brazil. Some of these were homestays which helped the CHI staff to experience what they were promoting to their local high schools. I also led CHI's first American student high school group to Japan, so I could have the experience of the new Sister School exchange program in person, and be able to train teachers, so that they would be effective tour leaders.

All of this experience led up to my being in charge of CHI's Russian high school homestay program here in the United States, and then in taking the first group from CHI to Russia, thus altering the course of my life once again. Meanwhile, Jim and I began to travel all over Europe, China, and Egypt and eventually cruised all over the world including the north Pacific Ocean from Japan to Alaska, and the North Atlantic from England to Iceland to New York as well as the Mediterranean Sea, the Baltic Sea, South America, Antarctica and to cruise all around the continent of Australia. The highlight of that trip was the private tour I arranged in Darwin with a local aboriginal gentleman.

I retired from CHI in 2000, and began my own travel business which I am still doing. I have always been curious about other cultures and languages. The best part of my travels are the people I meet, and the friendships I have made all over the world. I still keep in touch with Sten who is now 50 years old and is the father of two beautiful Swedish girls. I have several friends in Japan; Oshika *sensei* is one of them. He was the teacher-leader of my first Japanese group. We hosted him in our home, and have visited him in his home, both when his sons were very young, and again when his oldest son picked us up at the airport in Tokyo, and drove us to their home in Yokohama. Noriko was our first college-age student. We were invited to stay in her parents' home and her parents came to visit and stay with us. We attended her wedding in Tokyo a few years later. She now has two grown children. Shoji *san* was the friend of one of my students. I have lost track of the student, but Shoji *san* came to visit and stayed with us a short time upon the recommendation of my student, and has remained one of our fondest friends in Japan. He now has a grown family, a son and a daughter. And yet another past student, Chie married a Swiss man and lives in Vancouver, B.C. about halfway between their two families. Her daughter Kiara speaks four languages fluently: English, Japanese, German, and French.

We are still friends with our hosts from an adult exchange club in Australia, the Butlers, and they have been to our home as well. They recently met us at the cruise port near their home and spent the day with us. I keep in touch with Khalid, our incredible tour guide in Egypt. I was very worried about him during the riots in Cairo. I e-mailed him when I heard the news, and asked a very simple question: *Are you okay?* He e-mailed back and said: *Yes.* We have continued to correspond since then. We have kept it simple and light just in case he is being watched. During our river cruise on the Nile in 2006, Khalid had had an afternoon session with our group in which he talked about the politics, religious beliefs, and answered any and all questions we had. He is a very handsome, single young man, with an incredible knowledge of Egypt's ancient history, and imparted that information with a great sense of humor. We all adored him.

Little did I know when I was ten, eleven, twenty-one, or even forty years old that I would have the opportunity to see the world, and have such meaningful friendships with people of all cultures. Stassya's treasured friendship was the culmination of everything I have loved about meeting the people of our world. Building those bridges one-by-one is like climbing to the tallest peak and looking out over all the landscape. The view is breathtaking and worth every step of the way.

APPENDIX

Cultural Homestay International

Cultural Homestay International (CHI)
Toll Free: 1-800-432-4643
Website: chinet.org
CHI Blog | Facebook | YouTube | Twitter

Cultural Homestay International under Tom and Lilka Areton's love and care has grown over the years and changed with the times. They have many outbound and incoming programs.

American programs overseas:
AYP [Academic Year Program to study abroad in high school];
Au Pair;
Internship;
WE [World Explorers] sending hundreds of Americans overseas where they teach spoken, conversational English in exchange for room and board.

Programs incoming to the US:
AYP [Academic Year Program for high school students];
Camp Counselors [mostly UK participants];
SWT [Summer Work and Travel for university students from around the world who come to the US to work in resorts];
Internship/Trainee Program [serious professional training for overseas college graduates];
Au Pair;
GHP [Group Homestay Program (short-term)];
IEP [Intensive English Program for AYP high school students];
STEP [Student Travel Experience Program, volunteering in U.S.

nonprofits—one to three months].

Through their love of people, cultures, and languages, and their willingness to adapt, Tom and Lilka have influenced thousands of young people all over the world. Their influence grows even further when you factor in the families and friends to whom these young students return after being immersed in a one-on-one personal experience with other places and cultures whose lives are also changed in so many ways.

One of my Japanese students once told me, as we were saying goodbye at the airport: "I will teach my children how to hug as you have taught me." She and many other young students like her have taught me more about this precious world and the beautiful people in it than I can count.

Glossary

banana belt—A geographic area within a larger region that has warmer weather conditions and is more prosperous for agriculture.

Boris Yeltsin—The first freely elected president of Russia; ruled from 1991-1999.

Catherine II—Also known as Catherine the Great; ruled Russia in the second half of the 18th century; longest ruling female of Russia; expanded Russia's boundaries and granted some female rights.

Cold War—Began in 1945 with the end of World War II; political and military tensions between the United States (the ruler of democracy in the world) and the USSR (the ruler of communism in the world); these two countries never actually warred with each other but came close at least one time during the Cuban Missile Crisis of 1962.

Communism—A government that owns land, labor, and capital in the absence of human rights.

Communist Manifesto—Treatise written by Karl Marx in 1848; it's the political work that inspired Vladimir Lenin to turn Russia into a communist state.

Czar Nicholas II—The last Romanov king of Russia; he and his family were assassinated in 1917 during the Russian Revolution.

glasnost—Means "openness"; some freedoms and rights given to the Russian people in 1985 under the rule of President Mikhail Gorbachev.

hard currency—A foreign currency, like the US dollar, which is accepted anywhere in the world.

Iron Curtain—A term first used by English Prime Minister Winston Churchill to designate the boundary between democratic Western Europe and communist Eastern Europe from 1945-1991.

KGB—Organization similar to the Nazi Gestapo of World War II; known as the secret police for the Soviet Union from 1954-1991.

Kremlin—A multi-building complex located in Red Square; the seat of the communist government and the official residence of the leader of Russia.

Leonid Brezhnev—Ruled Russia from 1964-1982.

Marxism—The philosophy of Karl Marx which stated that people will overthrow their dictatorial governments and eventually create a government of total equality.

Mikhail Gorbachev—Eighth and last ruler of communist Russia; ruled from 1985-1991; responsible for the break-up of the USSR.

Nikita Khrushchev—Ruled from 1958-1964; during this Cold War period tension between the United States and Soviet Union was at its highest.

perestroika—Term associated with *glasnost* (see above); political, economic, and judicial changes within the Russian government.

Red Square—Moscow's centralized public square and marketplace.

socialism—A government, such as Russia, in which the government distributes resources, and in some countries people can choose their own profession, but all the industries are owned by the state.

Union of Soviet Socialist Republics—Also known as the Soviet Union; existed from 1917-1991, and included Russia, Tajikistan, Uzbekistan, and others in the same region.

Vladimir Lenin—The founder of communism in Russia and its first ruler.

White Nights—Natural phenomenon which lasts from June 11 to July 12 in the Arctic Region of the world, when the sun stays above the horizon, creating dim daylight twenty-four hours a day.

Made in the USA
San Bernardino, CA
29 November 2016